PURT NIGH GONE

Stroud & Hall Publishers
P.O. Box 27210
Macon, Ga 31221
www.stroudhall.com

The paper used in this publication meets the minimum requirements
of American National Standard for Information Sciences—
Permanence of Paper for Printed Library Materials.
ANSI Z39.48–1984. (alk. paper)

Library of Congress Cataloging-in-Publication Data

Miller, Zell, 1932–
Purt nigh gone : the old mountain ways / by Zell Miller.
p. cm.
ISBN 978-0-9796462-3-2 (pbk. : alk. paper)
1. Mountain life—Appalachian Region, Southern—History. 2. Appalachian Region, Southern—History.
3. Appalachian Region, Southern—Social life and customs. 4. Appalachians (People)—History. I. Title.
F217.A65M55 2009
975—dc22
2009007151

PURT NIGH
GONE

The Old Mountain Ways

To Steve
Best Wishes
Zell Miller
5/2009

Zell Miller

New York Times Best Selling Author

OTHER BOOKS

BY ZELL MILLER

The Mountains Within Me (1975)

Great Georgians (1983)

They Heard Georgia Singing (1985)

Corps Values (1997)

A National Party No More (2003)

A Deficit of Decency (2005)

The Miracle of Brasstown Valley (2007)

Dedication

With much love and gratitude, this book is dedicated to my wife
Shirley's parents: Luke and Bea Carver whose ancestors go back many
generations in the Great Smokey Mountains of North Carolina.

I have considered the days of old, and the years that are past.
—Psalm 77:5

Contents

Preface

As old Brasstown Bald Mountain looks down upon my valley home, Shirley, my wife of fifty-five years, Gus, our yellow Lab, and I stand along U.S. Highway 76, waiting to cross. It takes a while. The traffic is steady—more than 11,000 vehicles a day, I'm told.

As a child, I played hopscotch on that road with a rare car interrupting our game only every thirty minutes or so.

Less than an hour away, in a narrow slit of the North Carolina Nantahala Mountains, Rail Cove has a newly paved county road now running by Shirley's old homeplace. When her father and mother, Luke Carver and Bea, came there to live, the only way to get a vehicle into the area was to drive up the creek bed.

A few decades ago, Bob Dylan sang, "the times, they are a-changing." Today in our southern mountains, the changing has "advanced" to *vanishing*. That's what this book is about: a way of life that once was but is no more, a way of life that is purt nigh gone.

CHAPTER 1

In the Beginning

The world's largest, most varied, and probably first deciduous forest spawned, nurtured, preserved, and showcased within the world's most perfected, most picturesque, and probably oldest mountains.

That is what our Southern mountains are all about and why they are an irreplaceable natural resource we must protect and preserve for future generations.

God took his time in making these beautiful and unique mountains. Their story begins in the dim mists of Precambrian time, when the most advanced life form was primitive algae and from which the oldest discovered geologic formations found in Shenandoah National Park have been dated to more than eleven hundred million years ago.

The mountains rose a few inches a year over 50 million years from the collision of the North American and African tectonic plates, much as one sees today in the Sierra Nevada of California. The last great uplift pushed the Appalachians to the height of the Rocky Mountains, a cataclysmic event we have come to know as the Appalachian Revolution.

That occurrence created vast deposits of fossil fuels throughout Appalachia, rich coal beds, and even oil fields north in Pennsylvania. The subsequent 200 million years were centuries of eroding, leveling, faulting, and evolving that produced the beautiful, green, flowering mountains that today extend eastward and southward from the Gaspé Peninsula of Quebec to Northern Alabama. They reach their zenith in the great Blue Ridge that rises south of Harrisburg, Pennsylvania, and continues as both one main axis and divided ranges into North Georgia.

At the time of the Appalachian Revolution, the Arctic was warmer and the continents joined across Alaska and the North Pole.

Beginning some 70 million years ago during what is called the Tertiary Period of the Cenozoic Era, a vast circumpolar forest developed across that bridge with plants moving both to and from Eurasia and North America. The result of that transplanting is evidenced today by trees and spring flowers in parts of China that are much the same as in our Southern mountains and the leaf prints of magnolias in fossil remains in Canada and Greenland.

The Rockies were mere foothills and the peaks of Appalachia probably towered over those of the Alps when further movements within the earth separated the continents. Another 20 to 30 million years ago produced the rugged mountain chain extending from Canada to New Mexico that is the Rockies of today.

The rise of those new peaks and ridges cut off moisture from the west and rendered the central stretches of the North American continent too dry to support trees. This pushed the forest eastward to the point where it could thrive on rain carried inland from the Atlantic.

Then the Arctic turned cold and, about 1 million years ago, spread massive glaciers thousands of feet thick across the northern landscape. The ice extended into Pennsylvania and Ohio and bulldozed the forests it covered like some giant earthmover. Fortunately for future civilization, the North American mountains ranged from north to south, and the displaced trees could retreat before the flow of ice rather than being crushed into oblivion by it, as they were against the east-to-west ranges in Europe.

Thus, they survived to reestablish themselves on the receptive slopes and in the fertile valleys and isolated coves of our Southern mountains into what ecologists today classify as a "mixed mesophytic forest," writers refer to as an "Appalachian forest," and lumbermen speak of as "cove hardwoods."

The spruces, firs, and other conifers occupied the high ridges and peaks of our southern mountains, and the broad-leafed hardwoods and their storehouse of seeds survived in the protected valleys and coves. From the Cumberland Valley southward, the latter evolved into what the pioneer ecologist Professor Maurice Brooks of the University of West Virginia termed "a master experiment station," which achieved its greatest degree of development in the Great Smoky Mountains of North Carolina and Tennessee.

The fruits of this development can be seen today in the area we know as the Great Smoky Mountains National Park, where as many as 100 different species of trees—a number greater by 50 percent than that found in any other location on earth and more than on the entire European continent—have been identified growing in mutual and beneficial coexistence. There is not now nor has there probably ever been a richer or more varied deciduous forest anywhere.

As the climate reversed itself, the hardier of the species followed the retreating ice and replanted the devastated regions with forests of trees that could survive in the changed soil and weather environments. Thus, the New England heights became predominately coniferous, with spruces and firs on or near the summits and pines and hemlock down the slopes. The forests from the Catskills southward became increasingly deciduous until the broad-leafed, seasonal trees that flower in spring and flame in fall predominated and became prolific in the highlands of the Carolinas, Tennessee, and Georgia.

In addition, erosion and rising streams from our southern mountains seeded, planted, and watered the Atlantic Coastal Plain to the east, the Ohio and Mississippi River valleys, and, to a lessening degree, the plains and prairies to the west. Summits, ridges, plateaus, valleys, gaps, hollows, and coves were formed.

A gap is a low place in the main ridge of a mountain chain, almost V- or U-shaped in appearance. Some are former "water gaps" that have been left dry because of shifts in the mountains many years ago. Others are remains of small faults or weaknesses in the overlying rock. The soil is usually not as fertile, and the climate is harsher because of wind and ice storms. Over the centuries, wildlife from turkey to deer and bison have used the gaps for natural passageways.

Small short valleys between mountains are called hollows and geologically represent rock zones that were weaker and eroded faster than the surrounding highlands. They have a more moderate climate than the ridges and gaps. The hollows in the eastern slopes are cooler, and in the winter ice and snow lie longer there than on the hollows in the western slope because of the latter's longer period of afternoon sunshine. The mouth of the hollow has fertile soil while the sides are rockier. Old chestnut trees and hickories were usually plentiful in the upper hollows. There was also more plentiful wildlife in hollows.

A cove is somewhat similar to a hollow but with narrower walls and only one natural way in and out. The soil is the most fertile found in any geological formation, and a stream or streams form a narrow drainage outlet at the mouth of the cove. They are ideally suited for abundant wildlife year round. Indians often burned the coves, leaving small areas in the center and mouth of the cove to become grassy areas to attract wildlife.

The reforestation for which the Cumberland Plateau of Eastern Tennessee, Kentucky, and Southwestern Virginia served as the distribution center proceeded in three directions and compositions. The trees included birch, beech, and maple to the northeast, oak and hickory to the east and southeast, and oak and chestnut to the west.

But it was in the coves of our southern mountains that all the varieties met, flowered, and prospered. No one ever delineated the beauty and extent of it more fully or graphically than the premier chronicler of our southern mountains, Horace Kephart, in his enduring, best-selling book, *Our Southern Highlanders*, which has been in continuous print and circulation since 1913. He wrote,

> The richness of the Great Smoky forest has been the wonder and the admiration of everyone who has traversed it. As one climbs from the river to one of the main peaks, he passes successively through the same floral zones he would encounter in traveling from mid-Georgia to southern California.
>
> Starting amid sycamores, elms, gums, willows, persimmons, chinquapins, he soon enters a region of beech, birch, basswood, magnolia, cucumber, butternut, holly, sourwood, box elder, ash, maple, buckeye, poplar, hemlock, and a great number of other growths along the creeks and branches. On the lower slopes are many species of oaks, with hickory, hemlock, pitch pine, locust, dogwood, chestnut.
>
> . . . In this region, nearly all trees attain their fullest development. On north fronts of hills, the oaks reach a diameter of five to six feet. In cool, rich coves, chestnut trees grow from six to nine feet

across the stump, and tulip poplars up to ten or eleven feet, their straight trunks towering like gigantic columns, with scarcely a noticeable taper, seventy or eighty feet to the nearest limb.

Ascending above the zone of 3,000 feet, white oak is replaced by the no less valuable "mountain oak." Beech, birch, buckeye, and chestnut persist to 5,000 feet. Then, where the beeches dwindle until adult trees are only knee-high, there begins a sub-arctic zone of black spruce, balsam, striped maple, aspen and the "Peruvian" or red cherry. . . . Nowhere else in the temperate zone is there such a variety of merchantable timber . . . .

Kephart continued with this further vivid description of the undergrowth of the Appalachian forest, which he characterized as of "almost tropical luxuriance and variety":

Botanists say that this is the richest collecting ground in the United States. Whether one be seeking ferns or fungi or orchids or almost anything else vegetal, each hour will bring him some new delight. In summer, the upper mountains are one vast flower garden: the white and pink of rhododendron, the blaze of azalea, conspicuous above all else, in settings of every imaginable shade of green.

The illustrious botanist, William Bartram, on his plant-hunting trips into the mountains of western Carolina, discovered the fiery azalea and spread its fame throughout the world as "the most gay and brilliant flowering shrub yet known." As early as 1776, Bartram gathered plants along the Little Tennessee River, which he called "Tenase," and a Cherokee town called "Cowe." He also went into the deep gorge of the Nantahala River and met the grand chief of the Cherokees, Atakullakulla. He described the area as "a world of mountains piled upon mountains."

He also visited the area known today as the Joyce Kilmer Forest: 3,800 acres of old growth forests, some trees more than 400 years old. The forest was named for the *New York Times* writer who was killed in World War I and had written the well-known poem "Trees."

I think that I shall never see
A poem lovely as a tree.
A tree whose hungry mouth is prest
Against the earth's sweet flowing breast.

A tree that looks at God all day
And lifts her leafy arms to pray.
A tree that may in summer wear
A nest of robins in her hair.

Upon whose bosom snow has lain;
Who intimately lives with rain.
Poems are made by fools like me,
But only God can make a tree.

Renowned naturalist John Muir, as he hiked through North Carolina and Georgia in 1867, nearly a hundred years after Bartram, summed it all up with his observation that these forests "must have been a great delight to God, for they were the best He ever planted."

There were dinosaurs in our Southern mountains during the Mesozoic Era, and there have been significant discoveries of fossils along the Chattahoochee River in both Georgia and Alabama just south of the mountains. However, dinosaurs in this area do not appear to have been as large or numerous or to have played as major a role as in other parts of the North American continent.

There were some large mammals years later: mastodons, huge wolves, and bears much larger than today's grizzlies, big-horn sheep, caribou, elk, saber-toothed tigers, and large lions.

There were notable evolutionary developments in life forms in our southern mountains. This is attested by the fact that half of all the species of lungless salamander in North America have been discovered in our Southern mountains, some thirty-four different varieties. The area is a focal point in the study of those ancient creatures suspended in an anatomical warp between the gills of aquatic animals and the lungs of terrestrial animals.

Buried in the creek and river bottoms are also 300 species of mussel fauna, a third of the world's total. Quickly becoming extinct because of water pollution, these little creatures go through a stage as larvae and attach themselves to fish.

The trees and mountains in the south had achieved their finished grandeur long before the first white man first glimpsed them. Wholly unlike the raw, rugged, and barren peaks and ridges of the Alps, Andes, Himalayas, and Rockies, they are, with few exceptions, rounded and forested with few commanding peaks and only rare pinnacles or serrated ridges. Their first civilized visitors saw them, as did Horace Kephart, who wrote,

> From almost any summit one looks out upon a sea of flowing curves and dome-shaped eminences undulating, with no great disparity of height, unto the horizon. Almost everywhere the contours are similar: steep sides gradually rounding to the tops, smooth-surfaced to the eye because of the endless verdure. Every ridge is separated from its sisters by deep and narrow ravines. Not one of the thousand water courses shows a glint of its dashing stream, save where some far-off river may reveal, through a gap in the mountain, one single shimmering curve.

Most of the high points are in the 3,000-foot range, but there are several notable peaks in the Southern Appalachians. The tallest is Mount Mitchell in North Carolina, which stands at 6,685 feet and is clothed in spruce and fir. A close second is Clingmans Dome, which, at a 6,642-foot elevation, is the highest point on the Appalachian Trail, and those who climb its Frank Lloyd Wright-type observation tower can boast of being, at the moment, the highest earthbound persons in Eastern North America. Clingmans offers a special botanical feature in the dense stand of shrubby mountain cranberry, which flowers with pink shooting-star blossoms in spring and produces small rich red fruits in fall.

Because the trees of a deciduous forest shed their foliage in autumn and are reclothed in new dress in spring, two major byproducts of our southern mountain woodlands are the masses of wildflowers in spring and the dazzling colors of the changing leaves in fall.

Violets, anemones, hepaticas, phloxes, lilies, trilliums, and myriad other seasonal flowers burst forth when the warm sun of March and April strikes the earth beneath the bare and budding trees. It is a situation that develops sparsely, if at all, beneath the dense, permanent cover of evergreen coniferous forests. As many as thirty of the trees among cove hardwoods bear handsome blossoms with flowering periods extending from the snowy white blooms of serviceberry in March to the yellow flowers of the witch hazel in December.

A typical southern mountain cove's flowering plants of tree proportions would include, in addition, redbud, magnolias, tulip poplar, buckeyes, dogwoods, locusts, crabapple, mountain ash, black haw, yellowwood, fringe tree, silverbell, lindens, sourwood, and Hercules' club. In the borders between the trees and the shrubs are the rhododendron, mountain laurel, and azaleas, which grow in a profusion that can be described only as tropical.

Fall coloring differs from Northern to Southern Appalachia. The maples and birches blaze in the notches of New England in early October, while the vivid colors of the hardwoods and sourwoods progress down the spine of the great Blue Ridge through mid-November when the sweet gums of the deep South still flaunt their scarlet, purple, and gold.

A continuing mystery to ecologists, naturalists, and geologists alike are the eighty or so grassy islands called balds, which are found 4,000 feet and higher in the saddles between forested Southern Appalachian peaks from Virginia to Georgia. Mountain people have used them as summer grazing lands since settlers arrived in the mountains, and, although some suggest that either lightning caused them or Indians cleared them as places of worship, no concrete explanation more substantive than speculation ever has been offered for these lush alpine pastures.

They are made even more intriguing by the fact that the same three-toothed cinquefoil, a member of the rose family that is a native of the Gaspésian Highlands of Quebec, is also found on these balds, and the same snow buntings that feed on its wine-red seed capsules in Canada also appear to do the same on those of our southern mountains.

Further mysteries of the Appalachian coves are the many varieties of orchid species and exotic ferns found throughout the region: further throwbacks to climates and geologic eras lost in the dim pasts of prehistoric times when some ferns were as large as trees. Today there are more than a thousand herbaceous plants in Appalachia.

It is impossible to pinpoint the advent of man upon the scene. Early man may have been there at the time of glaciation, perhaps as long ago as one-half million years, but the aboriginal ancestors of today's Indians came on the scene less than fifty centuries ago.

It was not until close to 1700 that the English-speaking white men seriously penetrated the Appalachian wilderness. They came first in the form of hunters who left homes and families in the coastal plains to roam the uncharted wilderness for months at a time. The first settlers were the Palatine Germans. They came through Pennsylvania and settled westward as a buffer against the frontier for the Quakers in 1682.

The Scots-Irish Ulstermen, who fled English tyranny and the Irish potato famine, followed them. They eagerly took on the task of populating the colonial frontier and exterminating the Indians who resisted encroachment upon their hunting grounds.

There also were English, Irish, and French Huguenots among them, but the visionary, aggressive, quick-tempered, imperious Scots-Irish Presbyterians predominated. Justin Winsor described them as having "all the excitable character which goes with a keen-minded adherence to original sin, total depravity, predestination, and [who] saw 'no use in an Indian but to be a target for their bullets.'"

When western Pennsylvania became crowded, they pressed southwestward across the Potomac, up the Shenandoah, and into the western piedmont and foothills of Carolina. Numbered among these were the renowned frontiersman Daniel Boone and the ancestors of such future American greats as Davy Crockett, John C. Calhoun, Stonewall Jackson, and Abraham Lincoln.

A great early example of that spirit of independence was in 1772, *four* years before the Declaration of Independence, when a group of citizens on the Watauga River in North Carolina Territory drew up a resolution establishing a "Watauga Association" that created a code of laws with a court at its core. It was a democratic government in its purest form, independent of royal authority.

Watauga has been called the first free and independent government in America. It recognized no higher authority except God. It provided a five-man government with John Sevier, or "Nolichucky Jack" as he was called, as the chairman. They believed in swift and sure punishment for those who stole. All steps of the legal process, from arraignment, trial, conviction, and execution, they believed, could be done within an hour.

For horse thieves, the sentence went like this:

> It is ordered that they be confined in the publick pillory for the space of an hour, and that each of them have both of the ears nailed to the pillory and severed from their heads. That they receive at the publick whipping post, 39 lashes upon their bare backs, well laid on, and that each of them be branded upon their right cheek with the letter T, and that the sentence be put into effect between the hours of 12 and 4 this afternoon.

Sevier led his fellow frontiersmen, called the "Overmountain Men," at King's Mountain, North Carolina. It has often been called the turning point of the American Revolution. Before the battle, Sevier asked his several hundred men, "Does anyone wish to back out? If so, take three paces to the rear." When no one moved, Sevier asked again, "Do you understand? Just take three paces to the rear." One man replied, "Colonel, we can't move anyway but forward."

The battle went forward. Much of it was hand-to-hand combat, and it was over in less than an hour. The Americans lost 28 men with 62 wounded. The British had 1,100 killed or wounded, and the mountain no longer belonged to the king.

After the war, in 1785, Sevier was elected governor of what was called the State of Franklin. Finally, in 1793, this temporary fourteenth state became part of Tennessee, and Sevier was elected that state's first governor.

During the Revolution, the Appalachian frontier constituted lines of pioneer farms and settlements on the eastern and western slopes of the mountains. The interior of the highlands remained almost uninhabited by whites who sought better hunting grounds and homesteads than the mountains afforded. But as the rolling savannahs of the east and west became fenced and tilled and the large game exterminated or driven out, hunters and trappers from both the east and west began to move into the heart of the highlands and settle there.

By 1830, about a million permanent settlers of this frontier stock populated the eastern and western fringes of our mountains. They were not just poor whites descended from indentured servants. They were a radically distinct and even antagonistic breed who, as noted by Kephart in his book, had been "appropriately called the Roundheads of the South . . . [who] had little or nothing to do with slavery, detested the state church, loathed tithes, and distrusted all authority save that of conspicuous merit and natural justice."

Isolation and population pressures forced more and more settlers back along the creek branches and up the steep hillsides to "scrabble" for a living. Largely kept out were the "one-axle" characters, as they were sometimes called, who could not and the outlaws who would not make it over the mountains.

These early mountaineers were a special breed: a race of lean, inquisitive, shrewd, self-reliant, suspicious, primitive, and provincial people of the same descent who intermarried to a degree unknown in other parts of America. These traits spawned the unfair and unwarranted stereotypes of the "hillbilly" that still persist today with the slanders of comic strips like "Snuffy Smith" and television sitcoms like *The Beverly Hillbillies*. The real truth is that these people developed as a race of proud people of almost pure blood. They identified, by virtue of heritage, environment, and upbringing, more with their Elizabethan past than with the modern world outside their mountain coves. That outside world was one with which they had little communication and even less desire to emulate.

In Daniel Boone's day, the Eastern Highlands were populated with plentiful big game including the timber wolf, the puma, the eastern bison, and the eastern elk. All have since been rendered extinct by indiscriminate hunting and the zeal of sharp-shooting mountaineers to rid their world of "varmints."

Deer were so plentiful that deerskin became the equivalent of cloth, and the barter of their hides grew so prevalent that the word "buck" became synonymous slang for "dollar."

Napoleon Bonaparte's Grande Armée littered the snows of the Russian winter with Appalachian black bear pelts for which his purchasing agents paid the bounties that resulted in the gory slaughter to near-extinction of hibernating Appalachian bears in 1810. Bears, beavers, and deer have made strong comebacks in our modern southern mountains; the latter so much so that today's mountain residents often find themselves wishing for the reappearance of a few hungry pumas to cull the foraging herds. In 2001, an experimental release of twenty-five elk was begun in the Great Smoky Mountains National Park.

For a couple hundred years, many of these settlers were able to witness one of the wonders of the New World. Flocks of pigeons, sometimes a mile wide, could often blacken the sky for as long as four hours. There were a dozen or less flocks numbering hundreds of millions of birds, and they ranged from the East Coast to Montana, from the Gulf to Canada. They would come and go over Appalachia without warning. Often trees—entire forests—were nearly destroyed by their feeding and roosting habits. Entire "pigeon cities" 30 or 40 miles long would appear.

By the late 1800s, they had disappeared: shot and fed to hogs, their pigeon cities destroyed by bonfires dosed with sulfur. Females only laid one egg a year, and they obviously could not exist in their reduced numbers.

After the Civil War, there was indiscriminate cutting of the virgin hardwoods of Southern Appalachia to feed the growing nation's insatiable appetite for building materials. Hundreds of thousands of acres were cut bare of their virgin stands of ancient ash, beech, birch, chestnut, elm, hickory, hemlock, maple, oak, poplar, sycamore, and other varieties of hardwoods as well as pines, cedars, spruces, and other conifers.

This left the forests bare to the ravages of erosion and fire. The demand for coal to fire the furnaces of industry and the locomotives of the railroads not only brought the devastation of mining throughout the region, particularly in the Virginias, Kentucky, and Tennessee, but also resulted in the denuding of more forests to supply timbers to support coal tunnels. The area was also subject to huge landslides and devastating floods.

The indiscriminate removal of other mineral resources turned once verdant mountains into a moonscape, like the one in the vicinity of Copperhill, Tennessee, that only recently has become green again. All of this destruction of the fruits of nature produced over eons of evolution was further compounded by an Oriental blight in the 1920s that virtually destroyed Appalachia's incomparable and irreplaceable stands of stately chestnut trees.

The emerging forces of conservation and preservation, the growing knowledge of man's interrelationship with his environment, and the development of new and superior synthetic materials to supply the demands of human consumption helped save the indiscriminate exploitation of the natural resources of the southern mountains before and after World War II.

These ancient mountains have proven surprisingly resilient. They have withstood man and all the damage he could do with his years of burning, cutting, mining, leveling, filling, dynamiting, digging, damming, cementing, asphalting, and polluting. Somehow they spring back. Crosscut saws became power-driven chain saws; hammers became power nail drivers; backhoes became gigantic; plastic replaced paper; and still the mountains endure. Yes, the healing has become harder and takes longer, but it still goes on and will prevail.

But the mountain people? Their culture? Their old ways? Their language? They have not endured. They are purt nigh gone, and that's the subject of this book.

The Cherokees

The Cherokees were different and special.

They knew they were a breed apart and proudly called themselves the "Ani Yunwiya," which means "the principal people." White men who came in contact with them recognized and chronicled their exceptional physical, intellectual, and societal attributes, beginning with Hernando DeSoto in 1540.

Father Rogel, a Jesuit missionary who visited the Southern Indians with Spanish explorers in the 1560s, wrote that the Cherokees were "superior" to any Indians he encountered, and the early English explorer Henry Timberlake described them as "handsome and proud."

In his book, *Winning of the West,* Theodore Roosevelt asserted that the Cherokees were "a bright, intelligent race, better fitted to 'follow the white man's road' than any other Indians."

Anthropologists generally acknowledge that the Cherokees had an advanced culture that put them several notches above all other aboriginal Americans, with the possible exception of the Mayan and Aztec groups. Even that conclusion must be tempered by the fact that the Cherokees obviously possessed a capacity to adapt, evolve, and survive, while their Mayan and Aztec counterparts did not. The Mayans and Aztecs built pyramids, prized riches, made human sacrifices, resisted their invaders, and perished. The Cherokees built towns, established a government and a newspaper, believed in a Supreme Being, welcomed their visitors, and learned from them.

No aborigines in history were ever more quickly assimilated and civilized than the Cherokees. And, with the exception of the fate of European Jews at the hands of Nazi Germany during the Holocaust of World War II, no people ever paid a dearer price for their achievements than did the Cherokees in the "Trail of Tears," their forced relocation from their mountain homeland to the inhospitable territories of the American West.

The Cherokee tribe is most closely related to that of the Iroquois, and until recently it was believed that the two were ancestors of a parent tribe that dominated eastern North America from the St. Lawrence River to the Florida Everglades, with the two dividing the territory between the Iroquois in the north and the Cherokees in the south. Archaeological research by the University of North Carolina strongly suggests Cherokees lived in the area for at least four thousand years, and the Iroquois broke away about a thousand years ago. Subsequent to that, the coastal Indians left to become the Tuscarora, the largest component of the contemporary non-tribal confederation known as the Lumbee Indians.

Estimates of the number of Cherokees existing at the time of DeSoto range as high as 25,000 but generally fall in the range between 16,000 and 20,000. They lived in 60 or more villages encompassing a vast territory of some 40,000 square miles. It extended from the Ohio River on the north to the Tennessee River on the south and the Savannah River on the east. It embraced the Appalachian portions of the states of Kentucky, Tennessee, Alabama, Georgia, North and South Carolina, Virginia, and West Virginia.

The Cherokees were divided into seven matrilineal clans or families following the blood lines of the mothers known as Wolf, Deer, Bird, Red Paint, Blue Paint, Wild Potato, and Long Hair or Twister, each of which had a "mother" village and was represented in most of the other villages.

Each village had two chiefs—a White or Peace Chief, who directed domestic affairs concerning everything from spring planting to fall harvest, and a Red or War Chief, who commanded during winter, which was a time of war. Each village also had a seven-sided Town House (one side for each clan) where the residents met to decide community matters on a democratic, one-person-one-vote basis without regard to sex.

Each had its special group of leading females known as "War Women" or "Pretty Women" who wielded great influence in the determination of war strategy and made binding decisions on the fate of captives. Women were not subordinated in village life and, with the exception of such external concerns as war, hunting, and intervillage competition, had an equal voice in all matters and played dominant roles in clan regulations and the upbringing of the children. Cherokees traced their lineage through the female, and the male moved to the home and clan of the bride after marriage.

Each village was self-sustaining and largely autonomous within the loose structure of a confederation of four districts—"Overhill," "Lower," "Middle," and "Valley"—and the "Out" villages. Within each district, one of the strongest villages was informally recognized as the capital, and during times of strife, their chiefs met to plan concerted courses of action for the tribe.

A similar loose organization prevailed among the seven "mother" villages of the clans. The Overhill District capital of Chota on the Warriors Path through eastern Tennessee was the closest thing to a seat of tribal government until the Cherokee Nation was established and its capital located at New Echota near what is modern-day Calhoun, Georgia.

From time to time, one or another District Chief would emerge as the strongest leader of the Cherokees until 1792, when the Grand Cherokee National Council was organized and the "beloved man" Chief Little Turkey of Ustanali Village emerged as the first Principal Chief of the Cherokees and led the tribe until his death in 1807.

Unlike other American Indian tribes that were nomadic, lived in portable teepees, and followed game as a source of sustenance, the Cherokees established permanent, fenced villages of log and clay dwellings surrounding their town houses. They resembled the walled villages of medieval Europe or the frontier stockades built by pioneer white Americans. They planted, tended, and harvested crops in communal fields and demonstrated considerable sophistication in the art of cultivation. Fishing and hunting supplemented their produce.

Both men and women participated in the initial groundbreaking for yearly planting, and the women tended the crops while the men hunted, fished, repaired homes and fences, dug out canoes, and made blowguns and bows and arrows.

They organized their year around six major festivals: the First New Moon of Spring, the New Green Corn, the Green Corn, the October New Moon, the Establishment of Friendship and Brotherhood, and the Bouncing Bush. The latter two were designed for purification from past sins and hardships, cleansing of the village, homes, and selves for the new year, and the return and rehabilitation of past offenders who had escaped punishment by making their way to villages of "refuge," where their clans were not represented.

In keeping with their preoccupation with the number seven, every seventh year they had a seventh festival, the Uku Dance, marking the reinstatement or inauguration of the Principal White Chief.

The Cherokees also valued and enjoyed athletics and had a highly developed system of competition among the clans and villages in the game of "anetsa" or "stick ball." It roughly resembled and probably was an ancestor of our modern game of lacrosse. It was a rough-and-tumble, no-holds-barred game in which opposing teams sought to move a ball made of stuffed animal skin from the center of a measured field across goal lines at either end. They used small wooden sticks with netted ends for scooping, carrying, or throwing the ball. The only prohibition was that the ball could not be touched with the hands, and the levels of violent contact resulted in many severe injuries and even death. The first team to score 20 points won.

One form of capital punishment sanctioned by the villages was the so-called "honorable" type in which an offender was allowed to be killed in a "stick ball" game. The "dishonorable" type involved binding the condemned man and throwing him off a cliff.

Organized religion and formal worship were not major facets in the personal lives of Cherokees. They did not worship idols or personages but held to a belief system that parallels Christianity in many respects and made it easy for them to convert. They believed in a Great One who created heaven above and earth below and who would punish or reward human spirits after death. They revered nature in much the same way that Europeans believed in Christ, and, like Christians, they believed they were the principal people on earth.

Somewhere in their evolutionary past, the Cherokees discarded ritual, downgraded the role of priests, and developed a moral orientation characterized as the "Harmony Ethic," as opposed to the "Protestant Ethic." Essentially, it emphasized the freedom of the individual, minimized the need for formal controls, and stressed cooperation over competition and avoidance over conflict.

Whites were shocked by the considerable latitude Cherokees were permitted in personal behavior, a situation that caused many outsiders to regard Cherokees as juvenile because of their lack of personal constraints and promiscuous because of the ease with which they entered and left the marital relationship. Divorce was such a simple process under Cherokee practice that it could be achieved by the female merely placing the husband's belongings outside the dwelling or by the male merely moving out of the wife's house.

Because they were a gregarious people open to new ideas and wedded to a philosophy of getting along by going along, the Cherokees were victimized time and again by the white men from whom they sought to learn and whose civilization and ways they most wished to emulate.

Beginning with the hieroglyphic peace treaty signed with the English in 1684 down to the disastrous document that sealed their fate through forced removal in 1836, history records the Cherokees to have been the most "treated" Indian group in America. Not a single treaty they signed came close to being fully honored.

The price they paid for negotiating instead of fighting and compromising instead of resisting was the unrelenting encroachment upon and continuing annexation of their territory. At the time of their expulsion, the boundaries of the Cherokee nation encompassed less than half the lands they had embraced when the first white man came three centuries earlier.

Not only did they suffer the loss of their lands but also invasions by British and American troops and the militias of the separate states with which they shared common borders. Many of their number suffered the indignity of being captured and sold as slaves, and hundreds of others died from white men's diseases, particularly in the smallpox epidemics of 1739 and 1783.

The British carefully cultivated the friendship of the Cherokees. In 1730, they carried Chief Attakullakulla, who was known as "The

Little Carpenter," and a delegation of other Cherokee leaders to England to meet the king and sign a treaty of trade and friendship.

Although British troops joined the militia of South Carolina in driving the remaining Cherokees out of that colony in 1761, English ties with the Cherokees persisted into the American Revolution. Cherokees fought with the Tories against the American Rebels until the British were defeated at the Battle of King's Mountain in South Carolina in 1780.

American leaders in South and North Carolina, Virginia, and Georgia sent expeditionary forces from four directions into Cherokee Territory in 1776 and inflicted terrible losses upon the Cherokees. The best among them was left dead following the pitched Battle of Wyah Bald in the Nantahala Mountains, and more than fifty of their towns were burned, causing staggering property damage.

After this, Cherokee leaders sued for peace and in treaties signed with the four states ceded all their remaining land in South Carolina and everything in Tennessee to the Blue Ridge Mountains. They further agreed to supervision by an Indian agent to assure that they engaged in no further hostilities.

Fighting by diehards continued until 1785 with the most stubborn resistance coming from a group of Cherokee secessionists known as the "Chickamaugas." Under the leadership first of Dragging Canoe and later of half-breed John Watts, they established themselves on the Lower Tennessee River, and there they conspired against the American nation with Spanish agent Alexander McGillivrey and English soldier of fortune William A. Bowles.

The new American Republic under the Articles of Confederation sought to stabilize relations with the Cherokees with the Treaty of Hopewell signed in November 1785. Settlers, hunters, land speculators, and adventurers violated it before it was ever implemented.

When George Washington became the first president under the new United States Constitution, the Treaty of Holston was negotiated and signed on July 2, 1791. The treaty called for "perpetual peace and friendship" through fixed boundaries for the Cherokee nation guaranteed by the United States. It limited access to the territory by whites, prohibited against diplomatic agreements with either foreign powers or individual states, and paid an annuity of $1,000 that was later increased to $1,500. It also assigned representatives of the United States government working under the direction of the governor of the territory south of the Ohio to lead the Cherokee nation to "a greater degree of civilization, and to become herdsmen and cultivators, instead of remaining in a state of hunters."

The latter provision was the handiwork of Senator Benjamin Hawkins of North Carolina, who later served as an agent. He, along with Return Jonathan Meigs, who held the post from 1801 until his death in 1823, was one of the few white leaders who sympathized with the plight of the Cherokees. Hawkins gave genuine assistance in their determined endeavors to establish a model, independent nation in the American mold.

President Thomas Jefferson also took great interest in the Cherokees and their future. However, his involvement was not without deception. While encouraging the National Council to develop a structured government on the one hand, Jefferson at the same time negotiated the Georgia Compact of 1802, which committed the United States government to remove all Indians from Alabama, Georgia, Kentucky, North and South Carolina, Tennessee, and Virginia to lands west of the Mississippi River. Insofar as the states were concerned, the die was cast at that time, and events moved toward the forced removal of the Cherokees three and one-half decades later.

The year 1808 marked the official beginning of the Cherokee Republic with the election of Path Killer as principal chief by the National Council. It also established a permanent national police force named "The Light Horse Guard." This was followed by the creation of a national bicameral legislature in May 1817. It consisted of a Lower House, called the National Council, of thirty-two representatives. Four were elected from each of the eight districts. An Upper House, called the National Committee, was composed of thirteen members elected by the Lower House.

In 1823, a Supreme Court was established, and in 1827, only forty-six years after the ratification of the United States Constitution, a Cherokee National Constitution was adopted, patterned after the

American one, beginning with the following strongly familiar preamble

> We, the Representatives of the people of the Cherokee Nation, assembled in order to establish justice, ensure tranquility, promote our common welfare, and secure for ourselves and our posterity the blessing of liberty, acknowledging with humility and gratitude the goodness of the sovereign Ruler of the Universe affording us an opportunity so favorable to the design, and imploring His aid and direction in its accomplishments, do ordain and establish this Constitution for the Government of the Cherokee Nation.

The two men who were the principal protagonists in the events that led to the Cherokee removal were elected to the top legislative positions. They were Major Ridge as speaker of the National Council and John Ross as president of the National Committee. Ridge eventually conspired with the Andrew Jackson administration to draft, ratify, and implement a final treaty of removal. After exhausting every resource of opposition, Ross, as the fourth principal chief of the Cherokee nation, had the terrible task of leading his fellow Cherokees on their decimating "Trail of Tears."

John Ross, whose Indian name was "Cooseesoowe," was perhaps the foremost of the mixed-blood Cherokees who assumed major roles in the development of the Cherokee Nation and its government and culture. Others included George Guest or Sequoyah, who developed the famous Cherokee Syllabary that rendered the Cherokees nearly universally literate almost overnight; Charles Hicks, the national treasurer of the Cherokee nation; and Chief James Vann, the wealthy planter and entrepreneur whose home in Murray County is a Georgia historical landmark.

President John Quincy Adams publicly congratulated the Cherokee nation upon its new Constitution, and the new nation prospered after putting down a brief revolt led by Councilman White Path to repudiate it. There was stringent enforcement of the law, which made selling Cherokee land to outsiders a capital crime, a statute that resulted from the humiliation suffered by the tribe in 1775, when several chiefs sold all Cherokee territory in central and western Kentucky and parts of North Carolina to the Transylvania Land Company for 2,000 pounds and a log cabin filled with trading goods. The authority of the clans and the autonomy of the villages were slowly replaced with a national code of laws enforced by an elected national marshal and even a system of elected district judges and sheriffs.

The Cherokee thirst for knowledge led to the early acceptance of the schools of missionaries brought first by the Moravian Society of United Brethren in 1740, the Presbyterians in 1758, the Baptists in 1805, and the Methodists in 1822.

Although conversions were slow, the Moravians had great influence due to the support of James Vann. Their mission school tutored such important future Cherokee leaders as Charles Hicks, John Ridge, John Vann, and Buck Oowatie or Galagina, who later took the name Elias Boudinot and became the first editor of the Cherokee nation's famed newspaper, *The Cherokee Phoenix*.

Perhaps most influential of all was an interdenominational organization sponsored largely by Congregationalist-Presbyterian groups and Dutch Reformed Church elements. It was called the American Board of Commissioners for Foreign Missions and sent promising young Cherokee leaders to its Foreign Mission School in Cornwall, Connecticut, to prepare them for their future roles in the Cherokee nation. One of them was Boudinot, or "The Buck," as he was called, whose marriage with Harriet Gold, a white girl, resulted in their being burned in effigy and the closing of the school.

Of equal importance to the board's preparing of Boudinot as the printed voice of the Cherokees was its assignment of the Reverend Samuel Austin Worcester as one of its missionaries to Cherokee country. Worcester's arrest, trial, and conviction by the state of Georgia touched off the litigation resulting in the ruling by Chief Justice John Marshall and the United States Supreme Court in favor of the Cherokees. The ruling was defied by the state of Georgia and, more importantly, President Andrew Jackson.

The man who perhaps was more responsible than any other for the development of the Cherokee people as the most civilized, cultured, and best governed tribe of American Indians was not a chief or even one of the more renowned mixed-breed leaders, but the crippled, illiterate artist and silversmith named George Guest who was the half-breed son of an emissary sent to the Cherokee nation by President George Washington and whose Indian name was "Sikwayi" or "Sequoyah," which meant "possum in a poke."

Inspired by white men's manuscripts captured during the Creek Campaign of 1813–1814 in which he participated, Sequoyah boasted that he could develop "talking leaves" for the Cherokees and spent almost twenty years developing a Cherokee alphabet or syllabary of eighty-six characters, which looked like a combination of English, Greek, Hebrew, Egyptian, and Chinese letters and characters—one for each sound in the Cherokee tongue.

For his efforts, Sequoyah was ridiculed and accused of witchcraft; his wife burned his papers and his enemies burned his house. Cherokee elders generally dismissed him with patronizing amusement, terming his efforts "so many pheasant tracks criss-crossing each other in light snow." But things changed when he demonstrated before the National Council with his six-year-old daughter that any person who knew the Cherokee vocabulary and could memorize the syllabary could write and read the writing because there was no need to bother with spelling or syntax.

The council gave its blessing and in 1821 adopted the Sequoyah Syllabary as the Cherokee national language and thus inaugurated one of the greatest demonstrations of mass education in history. Sequoyah trained a cadre of young tutors who, in turn, held classes throughout the Cherokee nation. Soon every child and adult was studying and committing to memory his Cherokee characters.

Students who had labored two years in missionary school without learning how to write basic English were producing fluent Cherokee. The Sequoyah program came close to anticipating the future course of universal education in all of America and to being the forerunner of the phonics approach to teaching reading.

The Foreign Mission Board also perceived the significance of the new alphabet for the work of its missionaries and allowed Reverend Worcester to go to Boston with an appropriation of annuity funds from the Cherokee National Council to have the Cherokee language characters cast into type and to purchase a printing press for the Cherokee nation.

In October 1827, the National Council adopted a resolution establishing an official Cherokee national newspaper to be known as *The Cherokee Phoenix* and named Isaac N. Harris official printer for the Cherokee nation. The first five verses of Genesis were the first words to be printed in the Cherokee language and appeared in the December 1827 issue of *The Missionary Herald* in Boston.

Upon the arrival of the type and printing press in New Echota, Elias Boudinot was named by the council as editor of *The Cherokee Phoenix*, and he produced the first issue of the paper on February 21, 1828. The first three articles of the proposed Cherokee National Constitution were printed in the initial issue.

Things were never the same in the Cherokee nation. The dissemination of information played an important part in the events leading up to the Cherokee removal within the decade. It was limited only by the availability of paper and printing supplies and the difficulties of circulation.

Within six months, Boudinot was fired as editor because of his advocacy of "acceptance of removal with the best possible terms." Publication continued under a new editor, John Ross's brother-in-law, Elijah Hicks, until it went bankrupt and was discontinued with the issue of May 31, 1834. Until the end, Hicks preached encouragement of education as "the salvation of our suffering nation."

With its printing press, the Cherokee Council not only published its newspaper but also turned out a translation of the New Testament produced by Reverend Worcester and David Brown, a Cherokee who became a missionary to his people. They also prepared a spelling book and an official compilation of Cherokee laws.

The dissemination of the printed word to a nearly 100 percent literate population created the best informed and most cohesive public opinion ever achieved in any nation. Emissaries sent into the area from both the Georgia state and federal governments often found the Cherokee people better informed about the issues than they were. In fact, the Cherokee nation's press became such a potent weapon of public opinion that the Georgia state government seized it in 1835.

Accepting at face value all they had been told by every American president beginning with George Washington, the Cherokees sincerely pursued the overtures and encouragement of a benevolent United States government to follow "the white man's path" and for the first three decades of the nineteenth century probably made more progress than any people in history toward assimilating themselves into the culture of the white men around them.

They followed the advice of Thomas Jefferson to establish their own republican form of government, welcomed the official visit of President James Monroe, and took satisfaction in the approval of President John Quincy Adams of their new Cherokee National Constitution.

Having fought on the side of the United States in the War of 1812 and the Creek Uprising of 1813–1814 under the command of General Andrew Jackson, they erroneously assumed that Jackson would continue to be their friend after his election as president in 1828. They could not have been more mistaken. The Jackson administration's actions were their undoing, a fact that is particularly ironic since Cherokee Chief Junaluska saved Jackson's life in the Battle of Horseshoe Bend during the War of 1812. He was rudely dismissed by Jackson when sent to Washington as an emissary of the Cherokees.

Later, while on the Trail of Tears, Junaluska witnessed the death of a Cherokee mother with one baby strapped to her back and leading two other children by each hand. An eyewitness said Junaluska, with tears coursing down his cheeks, lifted his cap, turned his face to the sky, and cried, "Oh, my God, if I had known at the Battle of the Horse Shoe what I know now, American history would have been differently written."

Throughout the period of the height of the Cherokee nation's nineteenth-century greatness, there were continuing agitations for sections of Cherokee land. In 1817, a new treaty was negotiated that provided both for the subsidized relocation of Cherokees wishing to move beyond the Mississippi and the granting of 640 acres in the east to each Cherokee family whose members elected to become United

States citizens. Some 3,500 Cherokees enrolled to go west, Sequoyah among them, to join some 2,000 already there.

Two years later, in 1819, the treaty was amended to add to the western lands available to Cherokees in anticipation of a mass migration that never took place. More than 150 families opted for citizenship and touched off considerable litigation when whites claimed the same lands.

In addition to the election of Andrew Jackson, the year 1828 marked the discovery of gold in Cherokee territory. First, an Indian boy on Ward Creek sold a gold nugget to a white trader. Then, John Witherow and Benjamin Parks made their discoveries in what are now White and Lumpkin counties, respectively, and, by mid-1829, a gold rush brought some 10,000 gold-fevered prospectors into the eastern part of the Cherokee nation, particularly in the areas around what is now Dahlonega, Georgia.

The Cherokee National Council ordered the intruders out, but federal troops called in by Indian Agent Hugh Montgomery proved inadequate to the task. The Georgia General Assembly enacted a law extending the state's sovereignty over Cherokee territory on December 29, 1828, and petitioned President Jackson to remove federal troops, which he promptly did upon taking office.

The Georgia legislature also created a sixty-member Georgia Guard to control the area and prohibited the meeting of any Cherokee governmental body except to cede land. It also required the licensing of all white people, including missionaries, in the area and set up lotteries giving each white Georgia male "land" lots of 160 acres or "gold" lots of 40 acres.

Two missionaries, including Reverend Worcester, were arrested, tried, convicted, and imprisoned for being in the territory without licenses. Then, the Cherokee nation hired itself a Philadelphia lawyer, William Wirt, and took the whole issue to the United States Supreme Court.

Congress followed by passing a Removal Act on May 28, 1830, by the narrow margins of 28 to 20 in the Senate and 103 to 97 in the House. This law provided for the exchange of eastern Cherokee lands for comparable amounts of territory in the west to be negotiated.

Although few expected it to be implemented, President Jackson proceeded with the appointment of Benjamin F. Curry of Tennessee to serve as superintendent of Cherokee removal from Georgia.

The Supreme Court then ruled in the case of *Worcester v. Georgia* in February 1832 that all of Georgia's Indian laws were null and void and only the United States government could legislate for Indians. It ordered Worcester and Reverend Elizur Butler released and enjoined the state of Georgia from taking further actions against the Cherokees. However, President Jackson retorted, "John Marshall made that ruling, let him enforce it." He said the decision was an effort to embarrass him in an election year and urged his friend Georgia governor Wilson Lumpkin and the Georgia General Assembly to continue their anti-Cherokee activities.

Georgia proceeded to create Cherokee County out of Indian lands within its boundaries and provided for the election of officials to govern it from among Georgians living in the territory. Missionaries were ordered out of the area and their property seized, and Indians were dispossessed from much of the land won by Georgians in the land and gold lotteries.

Principal Chief John Ross opposed removal with every means at his disposal and was jailed on several occasions for his activities. President Jackson, realizing the matter never would be resolved in dealing with Ross, summoned him to Washington for consultations. At the same time, Jackson sent a New York clergyman, Reverend John F. Schermerhorn, to Georgia to negotiate a secret treaty with a minority group of Cherokees composed of Major Ridge and nineteen others.

Thus was the Treaty of New Echota drafted and signed in December 1835 by Major Ridge, John Ridge, Elias Boudinot, and Stand Watie, ratified by a one-vote majority in the United States Senate, declared law by President Jackson on May 23, 1836. It proposed a payment of $3,500,000 and a grant of 7 million acres in Indian Territory.

The Senate increased the amount to $5,000,000 after John Ross vainly sought a $20,000,000 settlement. The Cherokee National Council quickly rejected it, and a petition was gathered by Cherokee Vice Chief George Lowery that contained 15,904 Cherokee signatures or almost 100 percent of the 16,000 Cherokees believed living in the Eastern United States at that time.

The Jackson administration gave the Cherokee nation two years to remove its citizens west, and the Untied States Army disarmed them in August 1836. When the Cherokees made no voluntary efforts to relocate themselves within the allotted period, the new president, Martin Van Buren, ordered General Winfield Scott and a force of 9,500 U.S. Army Regulars to remove them forcibly.

Scott and his troops began rounding up the Cherokees and placing them in makeshift stockades exactly two years after the Removal Treaty became effective. Cherokees were arrested in their homes, fields, and everywhere they were found they were allowed to take only the belongings they could carry as they were placed in confinement.

No effort was made to identify or keep families together, and husbands and wives and parents and children were often separated and placed in different stockades. Impatient white mobs followed the troops, looting the abandoned Cherokee homes and villages. Hundreds died in the stockades before the westward trek ever began.

Bowing to the inevitable, Chief John Ross finally agreed to lead the exodus and, over the objections of former president Jackson, was made superintendent of Cherokee removal and subsistence and granted $65.88 per person to finance the trip.

Because severe drought made river travel impossible for all but an initial contingent of about 3,000, the approximately 14,000 Cherokees of the main body were moved overland in a 645-wagon caravan that began its journey at Murphy, North Carolina, in October 1838 and, winding its way through the five states of Tennessee, Kentucky, Illinois, Missouri, and Arkansas, ended at Tallaquah in what is now the state of Oklahoma on March 26, 1839.

A private soldier, John G. Burnett, who later rose to the rank of colonel in the Confederate Army, said his role was the "cruelest work I ever knew" and, on his eightieth birthday, described the privations that resulted in the deaths of more than 4,000 Cherokees in these moving words:

I saw the helpless Cherokees arrested and dragged from their homes and driven at the bayonet point into the stockades. And in the chill of a drizzling rain on an October morning, I saw them loaded like cattle or sheep into 645 wagons and started toward the west.

One can never forget the sadness and solemnity of that morning. Chief John Ross led in prayer, and when the bugle sounded and the wagons started rolling, many of the children rose to their feet and waved their little hands good-bye to their mountain homes, knowing they were leaving forever. Many of these helpless people did not have blankets, and many of them had been driven from their home bare-footed.

On the morning of November the 17th, we encountered a terrific sleet and snow storm with freezing temperatures, and from that day until we reached the end of the fateful journey on March 26, 1839, the sufferings of the Cherokees were awful. The trail of the exiles was a trail of death. They had to sleep in the wagons and on the ground without fire. And I have known as many as 22 of them to die in one night of pneumonia due to ill treatment, cold, and exposure. Among this number was the beautiful Christian wife of Chief John Ross. This noble-hearted woman died a martyr to childhood, giving her only blanket for the protection of a sick child . . . .

Somebody must explain the streams of blood that flowed in the Indian country in the summer of 1838. Somebody must explain the 4,000 silent graves that mark the trail of the Cherokees to their exile. I wish I could forget it all, but the picture of 645 wagons lumbering over the frozen ground with their cargo of suffering humanity still lingers in my memory.

But all of the Cherokees did not make the trip. Many of those living in North Carolina were the beneficiaries of an exemption negotiated by their white legal counsel, William Thomas, whereby they were allowed to remain in return for their acceptance of the sovereignty of the state of North Carolina over their villages.

Joined later by other Cherokees who eluded General Scott's dragnet by hiding out in the mountains, their total number was about 1,000, and they were the forerunners of the recognized tribe of Eastern Cherokees currently inhabiting what is known as the Qualla Boundary Reservation in western North Carolina, which they have developed into a highly profitable tourist attraction centered around Cherokee, North Carolina.

Of the 4,000-plus Cherokees who perished in the relocation, some 1,600 fell on the Trail of Tears, and the remainder died either in the stockades before the trip or of the hardships in their new homeland afterward.

There was strife between Cherokee leaders who accepted and those who opposed the removal. Most of the former met violent deaths, including Elias Boudinot who was assassinated. John Ross continued as principal chief, and his reign spanned four decades.

The western tribal status was terminated at the turn of the century, and there was an effort to do the same with the eastern group in the 1920s. This resulted in many whites endeavoring to purchase Cherokee status and giving rise to the term "Five Dollar Indian," but it came to naught when their status was changed from a state corporation to a federal reservation. Currently more than 5,000 Eastern Cherokees live on the North Carolina Reservation, and more than 50,000 others live in the west, mostly in Oklahoma.

CHAPTER 3

Gold in the Hills

"Thar's gold in them thar hills."

The general perception is that this was the cry of gold-fevered prospectors of the 1849 California Gold Rush. This myth had its genesis in the colorful prose of Mark Twain's book, *The Gilded Age*, and then it was romanticized by the movie industry, which has never let the facts stand in the way of a good story.

The truth of the matter is that the words stem from the impassioned plea of Dr. Matthew F. Stephenson, assayer of the United States Branch Mint at Dahlonega, Georgia. He urged Georgia gold miners to stay with the known quantity of Georgia's gold fields rather than being tempted by the unknown quantity to be found in California. Dr. Stephenson was an amateur geologist and self-appointed one-man chamber of commerce. So convinced was he that Georgia was one of the richest mineral states in the nation that he stood on the balcony of the Lumpkin County Courthouse in Dahlonega, gestured broadly in the direction of Findley Ridge half a mile to the south, and declared, "Why go to California? In that ridge lies more gold than man ever dreamt of. There's millions in it!"

The good doctor's rhetoric was more memorable than persuasive. In less than a decade, Findley Ridge was to become the site of what probably was the richest single gold strike in Georgia. It was known as "The Findley Chute," and the miners, while not heeding Stephenson's advice, did not forget his words and made the expression "There's millions in it!" their rallying cry in the face of discouragements and setbacks in California. Whenever a claim seemed barren and the prospector began talking about giving up, the Georgians would rally his resolve and spirit by pointing to the claim and exclaiming, "There's millions in it!"

A man named William Sellers, who had joined the company of the Georgia prospectors, was intrigued by the practice and reported it to Twain, who was collecting and recording the stories of the California gold fields. Attributing it to a semi-fictional character he called Colonel "Mulberry" Sellers, Twain incorporated the tale into his book and thus gave worldwide coinage to the practice and the cry as Californian in concept.

Over the years, the words "There's millions in it!" became the more flamboyant "Thar's gold in them thar hills!" But folklore and film have largely obscured its Georgia origin. The true story is to be found in the excellent little book, *Auraria: The Story of a Georgia Gold-mining Town,* published in 1956 by the renowned historian, the late Dr. E. Merton Coulter, who for many years was head of the Department of History at the University of Georgia.

Twain also missed the story of Georgia's "Russell Boys"—William Green, Levi, and Oliver—who left Lumpkin County in 1858 to prospect the eastern slopes of the Rockies and touched off the century's third major gold rush with their strike at Cherry Creek in the shadow of Pike's Peak in Colorado. They founded a town there that they named after Georgia's Auraria, which means "gold mine" in Latin. Later, the settlement combined with and took the name of the town on the other side of the stream called "Denver."

Neither did Twain record the fact that another Georgia prospector, John Hamilton Gregory, was the man who on May 6, 1859, discovered near the Russells' diggings what came to be known as the Gregory Lode. Once described as "the richest square mile on earth," this was the greatest single gold strike in American history.

Twain also failed to report the exploits of the company of Georgia miners led by Franklin Paschal of Auraria, who marched to help Texans win their independence and to avenge the deaths of their fellow Georgians, James W. Fannin and his 300 followers, who had perished in the massacre at Goliad in 1836.

Those are but a few of the failures of history to give full credit to the impact of the discovery and mining of gold upon the growth and development of our southern mountains. That is particularly true of the state of Georgia, where the economic, social, and motivational impact of the precious yellow metal was the greatest. As previously pointed out, it was perhaps the major factor in the tragic expulsion of the Cherokee Indians from the state.

Gold was discovered and mined in commercial quantities over a wide area of the eastern slopes of the Great Blue Ridge extending from western Maryland through northeastern Alabama. Several rich finds were made around Charlotte, North Carolina, and four major belts were discovered in Georgia. The richest was the Dahlonega Belt, which extends about 150 miles in length to varying widths of 2 to 6 miles. The other three are the Hall County Belt, the Carroll County Belt, and the McDuffie County Belt, with the latter claiming to be the site of the first discovery of gold in Georgia in 1823.

The when, where, and who of the first discovery of gold in Georgia will never be definitely known. Chief Ozley Bird Saunook of the Eastern Band of Cherokees stated in 1955 that his people had known about the gold in and around Dahlonega from the time of DeSoto in the sixteenth century. W. Larry Otwell, in his book, *The Gold of White County, Georgia,* said his research on the subject led him to the conclusion that "the Cherokees were the original finders of the yellow metal they called 'dalonigei.'" He wrote that, while there were no archaeological proofs of the fact, he found it "inconceivable that thousands of Cherokees, established in their villages along auriferous streams, failed to notice the bright metal that littered the stream beds." One can only theorize, therefore, that the Cherokees never placed the value on gold that white men did, and they kept quiet about its presence because they realized the turmoil its discovery would entail.

Depending upon what book or whose memory one accepts as authoritative, and not pursuing the McDuffie County story since this is a book about our southern mountains, the discovery of gold that touched off the Great Georgia Gold Rush of mid-1829 came about in one of three ways.

One is the sale of a gold nugget by an Indian boy living on Ward's Creek in Cherokee Territory to a white man named Jesse Hogan, who later claimed he found it. The second story is the kicking up of a gold-bearing quartz rock by Benjamin Parks while hunting deer near the site of what was to become the famed Calhoun Mine in Lumpkin

County. Mr. Parks himself recalled this story in an interview with the *Atlanta Constitution* on his ninety-fourth birthday. The third story is that John Witherow (or Witheroods) found a three-ounce gold nugget on Duke's Creek. This site was to become the celebrated Nacoochee Mine in what was then Habersham and is now White County near the present mountain resort town of Helen.

The Parks claim probably has received more attention because it came from the living lips of the claimant as well as because it is a documented fact of history that Parks later sold his mining lease to former vice president and United States senator John C. Calhoun of South Carolina.

Calhoun gave the mine his name and partnered with his son-in-law, Thomas C. Clemson, who was a mining engineer. They used slave labor from Calhoun's plantation at Pendleton, South Carolina, and it "made a mint of money" for them both. The size of the fortune made by Calhoun is not precisely known, but it is documented that the mine was one of Georgia's richest and produced 24,000 pennyweights (a pennyweight being 1/20th of an ounce) of gold in its first month of operation. It also is a matter of record that Clemson used much of his part of the fortune to found and endow the famed South Carolina university that bears his name.

It was also Calhoun who, with the help of his equally colorful colleague, Missouri senator Thomas Hart Benton, known as "Old Bullion," got a $50,000 appropriation through Congress to establish a branch mint in Dahlonega in 1837. Machinery was hauled laboriously overland from Savannah, and the mine began operation the following year.

From that time until it was seized by the state of Georgia at the beginning of the Civil War in 1861, it recorded receipts of $6,115,569 over and above the $1,763,900 received by the parent Philadelphia Mint from 1828 through 1837.

Those figures represent only a fraction of the total amount of gold believed extracted from the Georgia fields because much of it was coined through private mints like that established by Templeton Reid in Gainesville or shipped out by the branches of the Bank of Darien. This bank, headquartered on the coast, established these branches first in Auraria and then in Dahlonega. Also, it is believed that both European investors and Americans shipped large amounts abroad.

Dr. Stephenson, who was sometimes given to exaggeration, estimated the value of gold mined in Georgia from 1829 to 1839 at $20 million. This is a figure repeated by the Georgia historical marker placed at the site of Auraria in 1954.

Dr. Coulter, working from all estimates available to him, placed the figure at $16,000,000 extracted from 1829 to 1896, and Dr. S. P. Jones, assistant Georgia state geologist, put the figure to 1909 at $17,500,000. Whatever the amount, tremendous fortunes were made and lost.

The Dahlonega mint struck $5.00 gold coins known as "Half Eagles" that bore the distinctive "D" of the logo it adopted to mark its coinage. It later produced a full range of denominations of which only six sets are known to be in existence today. One of them is owned by North Georgia College and is valued at $40,000.

The Reid Mint in Gainesville turned out $2.50, $5.00, and $10.00 gold coins, which were determined by assayers to be worth more than their face values. Today, coins are so rare that only six of the $5.00 pieces are documented as still in existence, and one once sold for half a million dollars. Even rarer are the coins Reid struck after relocating his mint to California during the gold rush there.

The mint's machinery rusted beyond repair during the Civil War, and the building was used as a school for black children of the community until the Freedman's Bureau erected a new one for them in 1871. Congress then donated the structure and its site to the state of Georgia for educational purposes. In 1837, the parent institution of what is now North Georgia College was opened as one of the nation's first military land grant colleges. It set a further precedent in being coeducational from its inception.

The original mint building burned to its granite foundations on December 29, 1878, and the present Price Memorial Administration Building, named in honor of its founder, Colonel and Congressman W. P. Price, was erected on those stones. It is topped with a steeple, which was gilded with 14 1/2 ounces of native gold pressed 250 thousandths of an inch thick over its 6,888-square-foot surface in celebration of the college's centennial year.

Only two buildings in the world are so adorned. The other is the Georgia State Capitol, which had its classic dome embellished with gold mined by the people of Lumpkin County and transported to Atlanta by covered wagon train.

The town of Auraria was a microcosm of America's first gold rush with its boom and bust. That it has been portrayed in fiction and memory as the original booming, sinful mining town that set the pattern for such places in the American West is largely due to the vivid imagination of Charleston novelist William Gilmore Simms and his bestselling book, *Guy Rivers: A Tale of Georgia,* as were the even more colorful events of the California Gold Rush sensationalized by the pen of Mark Twain.

In comparison with those of the West, Auraria was a law-abiding town. The facts of its history make clear that it was not a prototype of the fast, loose, and lawless settlements that made wide-open, riotous saloons, shootouts in the streets, and vigilante justice their hallmarks. Even Simms, who visited the area fifteen years after the fact of his book, had to admit that he did not so much as see a drunk, to say nothing of witnessing a fight or hearing of a cockfight or gander pulling. Nevertheless, the fictional fiend he created in 1833, Guy Rivers, continues to have a life of his own as a cunning criminal who terrorized gold diggers from a hideout in a wild cave on a cliff overlooking the Chestatee River.

This is not to say there were not rowdy and wide-open places in the mountain area at the time. Sixty years after the gold rush ended, Colonel W. P. Price remembered, "Gambling houses, dancing houses, drinking saloons, houses of ill fame, billiard saloons, and tenpin alleys were open day and night." He called Saturday nights particularly "hideous" and observed that both women and men were "equally vile and wicked."

Auraria had its beginning in summer 1832 when a squatter, William Dean, built a cabin on the ridge separating the westward-flowing Etowah and the southward-flowing Chestatee rivers by only two miles. It was a natural congregating point for the swarms of prospectors who invaded the waters of those two rivers and their tributary streams with pans, spades, and rocker cradles.

Dean was followed by entrepreneur Nathaniel Nuckolls, who set up a small tavern that catered to the thirst of the miners for strong ale. The tavern was first called Deans and later Nuckollsville. It then began to be called and spelled "Knucklesville" because of the habits of drunken miners to settle their disputes with their knuckles.

Within the year, three leaders came to the community and gave it its name and character. The first was Mrs. George W. Paschal, or "Grandma Paschal" as she was affectionately called. She was the widow of a Revolutionary War soldier from Oglethorpe County and brought her family with her. She bought out the Nuckolls' establishment and set up a tavern, as she put it, "to entertain in a comfortable manner." In other words, no alcoholic beverages were served. A moral and religious woman, she also proceeded to establish a Baptist church and to become known as the "Angel of Auraria" for her ministrations to the sick and needy.

The second was John C. Calhoun who established his mine on the claim he purchased from Benny Parks and who was determined to see that Auraria became a proper, dignified community worthy of the presence of a senator and former vice president of the United States. He set about to find a better name than "Knucklesville" and endorsed adoption of the one proposed by his South Carolina colleague, a Doctor Croft, who advocated the town be named Aureolo, meaning "golden" or "shining like gold," and the county Aldoraddo, which he said was Spanish for "gold region."

The third individual, an entrepreneur and community leader named Major John Powell, came up with the name Auraria, which he said was Latin for "gold mine." The name Auraria stuck, although the official designation of the settlement remained Lumpkin Court House until the county seat of Dahlonega, six miles away, was established in October 1833. It was carved out of Cherokee, Habersham, and Hall counties. In 1832, the Georgia General Assembly named the county for the incumbent Georgia governor Wilson Lumpkin in recognition of his role as the prime mover in ridding the area of the Cherokees and establishing the ownership of their lands by lottery. He had been a congressman and was a friend of President Andrew Jackson, who shared his view that the Indians should be removed.

Lumpkin had strongly supported the lottery, which was held in October 1832. The previous governor, George Gilmer, had opposed it. One could choose from two different kinds of lots. There were gold lots of 40 acres each and land lots of 160 acres each. The lottery was extremely popular with the people. In the gold lot lottery, 133,000 names were registered for 35,000 lots, and 85,000 registered for 18,309 lots.

To qualify to register for either, one was required to have been in the state of Georgia four years for the land lots and three years for the gold lots. Cherokees could not participate. Only white males of eighteen years or over, widows, the deaf, dumb, and blind, and families of orphans consisting of more than two were eligible.

By 1834, Auraria had a population estimated at 1,000, although some estimates put it as high as 4,000 and that of the county at 10,000. At that time there were a hundred dwelling houses, twenty stores, five taverns, three physicians, three tailors, a branch of the Bank of Darien, a newspaper of acclaimed journalistic excellence called *The Western Messenger*, and more than two hundred gold mines.

There were also fifteen lawyers, testimony to everyone's preoccupation with land titles and the litigation resulting from them. Disputes that would have been settled with guns in the streets of the West wound up in court in the Georgia gold fields, and only one murder is recorded in the annals of Auraria.

One of the reasons assigned to the choice of Dahlonega over Auraria as the county seat of Lumpkin County was the number of disputed land titles growing out of the fact that a family of orphans living in Newton County drew, in the Georgia Lottery, the lot on which Auraria was situated. The lots were sold at "public outcry" in November 1833 and brought a total of only $2,089 because of skepticism about Auraria's future. There were a number of lawsuits over the failure of some buyers to complete their transactions and occupants of the lands to pay rents assessed by the orphans' guardian.

Clouded land titles, litigation, uncertainty about the town's future, the flimsy construction of its buildings, and its failure to become the county seat began the descent of Auraria. The California Gold Rush of 1849 accelerated and sealed its demise. The fast exodus of miners to the West coupled with that of business and governmental affairs to Dahlonega reduced the population of Auraria to less than three hundred. When Grandma Paschal's son George returned from Texas for a visit in 1858, he noted the town had "fallen into decay."

The Georgia Gazetteer of 1860 did not even consider Auraria important enough to be described and included it only in a list of post offices. Grandma Paschal continued to live there and, after her death in 1869 at the nearby home of one of her daughters on the Etowah River, she was buried in the Auraria Baptist Cemetery beside the remains of her husband, which she had had removed there at the height of Auraria's boom. Today, the monuments marking their graves and the nearby church are, with the exception of Georgia's historical marker, nearly all that remains to mark the glory that once was Auraria and the memory of Georgia's most famous ghost town. As Dr. Coulter concluded in his book, "Auraria was a phenomenon. Excitement had produced it; excitement was to end it."

The city of Dahlonega, though not as colorful in origin as Auraria, certainly has been equally colorful in longevity. Its name is derived from the Cherokee word for gold, and it went through a series of spellings ranging from "Tahlanauneca" to "Talonaga" until the pronunciation and spelling were corrected by a Cherokee Indian with a classical education who said it should be "Dahlohnega." The founding fathers dropped the second "h" and went with Dahlonega.

The city's first claim to fame was as a small clearing where Benny Parks and Lewis Ralston had a "licklog" to salt their colts and then as a campsite for hundreds of miners. When the five justices of the governing Inferior Court of Lumpkin County chose it as the county seat, its first permanent building was a log cabin built to house the sessions of the Superior Court.

The first contractor to build a permanent courthouse defaulted in 1834, and the second one completed the project in September 1836, reportedly putting a Bible under each of the four cornerstones and building it of bricks made from local clay, which, it is said, still glimmer when sunlight plays across their flecks of gold at certain angles.

The structure is the oldest standing permanent building in North Georgia. It now houses the popular Georgia Gold Museum, which is the centerpiece and principal tourist attraction of Old Dahlonega and was restored to its earlier grandeur as part of the nation's Bicentennial Celebration.

The city reputedly sits atop a fabulously rich gold vein, which never has been more than peripherally tapped. The saying that Dahlonega is the only city this side of heaven which literally can boast of having "streets of gold" is based on the fact that in the late 1800s, an excavation in one of the city's main streets uncovered a vein of gold two feet thick and "very rich" from which the city council removed several pounds of ore for display at one of the major turn-of-the-century expositions in Atlanta.

There is also the story of the famed Smith House being situated atop another such vein, which stems from the often-told tale that its builder, a wealthy gold miner named Frank Hall, discovered a vein several feet wide and of unknown depth while digging the basement for his new house in Dahlonega. Having all the money he wanted or needed and not wishing to contend with the furor he knew would result or chance the destruction of half of the town, it is said that Hall decided to cover up his find and forget it.

The first mining in Lumpkin, White, Habersham, Hall, and surrounding counties was done by individuals digging up and washing out the sand and gravel of the banks and beds of streams and the sides of adjacent hills. Their diggings transformed the hinterlands of Auraria and Dahlonega into a pitted landscape. The diggings grossly altered the courses of many of the branches and tributaries of the Etowah and Chestatee rivers.

The typical miner, depending upon shovel, pan, and rocker cradle, was lucky to average five to ten pennyweights of gold a day, barring the good fortune of finding a big nugget or discovering a rich vein. The process was both inefficient and wasteful, and even those who could afford and did use some of the primitive and expensive washing machines that were peddled at the time could boast of capturing no more than 50 percent of the gold present in the dirt and rock they handled. The situation called for capitalized mining companies and a modern, mechanized process for extracting the parent veins and rich placer deposits of gold that lay deep inside the mountains and produced, through erosion, the gold dust and nuggets that individual prospectors panned out in the beds of the streams that cut through the valleys.

The void was filled in 1834 with the chartering of the Pigeon-roost and Belfast Mining companies. The two were capitalized with unprecedented stock sales totaling $400,000 and $500,000, respectively. Scores of other companies, including the closely held enterprise of John C. Calhoun, were established to bring the full range of nineteenth-century technology to bear in extracting the riches of the North Georgia hills.

These firms developed a pioneering technique of hydraulic mining, which was written up in all the mining textbooks thereafter as the "Dahlonega Method." It involved the displacement of gold from the sides and tops of the mountains through the power of water sprayed upon them through pressurized pipes in much the same way that modern fire hoses extinguish fires in high-rise buildings and at other inaccessible sites.

Pipe was laid for miles into the mountains, the longest stretch being for a distance of twenty-nine miles. Hikers in the hills still stumble upon sections of the old, rusting pipe. The streams of water thus played upon the mountaintops literally washed the gold-bearing rocks, gravel, and dirt into the valleys. There they were crushed in monstrous stamping mills and then washed over mercury-coated plates that attracted and held the gold. The vibrations from the stamping mills in full operation were said to literally shake the mountains like earthquakes.

Another sensation of the times was the appearance and operation of history's first diving bell from a boat launched on the Chestatee River near Auraria in early 1833. There is no record of how much, if any, gold was retrieved from the sands of the bed of the Chestatee in that fashion.

Hard facts on the production and income from individual mines are difficult to come by. What is known is based largely upon hearsay. John C. Calhoun never revealed any figures about the fortune he earned from the Calhoun Mine, and it is ironic to note that this site was the last reported major gold strike in Lumpkin County. More than 110 years after Benny Parks first kicked up the rock that started it all, the entrance to the mine tunnel was enlarged in 1939, and a rich vein of gold was discovered just under the path trodden hard by miners for a century. Major G. C. Dugas bought the lease, put out the word that the strike was worth perhaps $40,000,000, took money from a large number of investors, and then left town.

The Findley Chute is believed to have made more than a quarter of a million dollars for Colonel J. J. Findley and his partner, Harrison W. Riley, before it came into the hands of the W. Reese Crisson family who moved to Georgia from North Carolina. The Crissons not only worked it but also the Lockhart, the Ryder Lead, and the McGee Arm mines. Later they purchased holdings north of Dahlonega.

Reese's grandson, John W., upon his retirement from military service, turned the latter Crisson Mine into a major tourist attraction by opening it to the public, charging admission, and renting equipment to private citizens wishing to try their luck at panning for gold. Rookie prospectors are allowed to keep all the gold they find. The other Lumpkin County operation still in existence is that of the Gold Hills of Dahlonega Mine.

In addition to the Gold Street Mine inside the city of Dahlonega to which I referred earlier, some of the more famous operations of history included

- the Free Jim Mine, operated by an emancipated Negro named James Boisclair who became wealthy, established a mercantile store and saloon in Dahlonega, and went to California where he was shot and killed in a miner's quarrel during the California Gold Rush.
- the Battle Branch Mine, which made a fortune for Major John Hockenhull of Dawson County after Georgia miners successfully defended it against a group of Tennessee hog drovers in a pitched battle in which one man was killed and many wounded.
- the Boling W. Fields Pocket, which was the richest top pocket found in the Dahlonega Gold Belt, discovered by Boling W. "Boley" Fields in the bed of the Chestatee River; from it he took an estimated 96,000 pennyweights of gold before losing the claim in litigation.

• the Preacher Mine of J. L. Wallace and Robert Howell, which produced the largest and purest nuggets of any mining operation in the area. There was one recorded instance of less than one peck of quartz yielding 195 pennyweights of pure gold.
• the Nacoochee Mine, which was White County's principal operation on the site of the Witherow strike on Duke's creek near Helen.

Of all the documented fortunes made in Dahlonega gold, the greatest probably was that realized by Samuel J. Tilden, the man who lost the presidency to Rutherford B. Hayes by one vote in the electoral college of 1876. He bought the holdings of former president Ulysses S. Grant, William Windom, and others for $500,000 and proceeded to make more than $4,000,000 from 16,000,000 tons of ore, which he washed out of his claims with water carried through a ditch thirty miles long he had dug for the operations. He sold out to S. L. M. Barlow, who made another $3,000,000 before, in turn, selling out to the ill-fated Dahlonega Consolidated Gold Mining Company.

"Consolidated" was one of four companies capitalized to take advantage of what was believed to be a new gold boom in the early 1900s. It was capitalized at $5,000,000, as was the Standard Gold Mining Company of Dahlonega. They were joined by the Crown Mountain and Briar Patch Gold Mining companies, with stock sales of $2,500,000 and $2,000,000, respectively. All lost fortunes, and Consolidated went bankrupt in 1906.

Although there have been flurries of excitement like the Dugas machinations with the old Calhoun Mine, the glory days that were the pre-Civil War boom times of North Georgia Gold Country have never come close to returning. Today's gold is mined from the pockets of tourists and affluent outsiders who build summer and retirement homes throughout the North Georgia mountains.

It would be interesting to know what the ghosts of Auraria and "Licklog" think about what is happening today on the ridges where they sought fortunes and became legends.

CHAPTER 4

The Way Life Was

In the sophisticated circles of modern society, people have always shown great interest in encouraging knowledge and preservation of various ethnic cultures. Much time and millions of dollars have been spent studying and praising civilizations like those of the Indians of the American West, the Polynesians of the Pacific Islands, the Aborigines of Australia, the Cossacks of Russia, and similar groups around the globe. Perhaps the most intriguing of them all is that of the white Scots-Irish-Celtic settlers of our rugged and remote southern mountains.

The tendency to extol the colorful aspects of provincial customs and quaint lifestyles of different races and habitats rarely extended to those who, but for the isolation of geography, might have evolved outward rather than inward. Perhaps the explanation for this long delay is that of a reverse mirror-image syndrome, which causes those who regard themselves as superior to revile rather than revere that which they might have been but for the accident of places of birth.

For whatever the reason, the course of most has been to ridicule the "hillbillies" and their "backward ways" and to view with condescension their unique culture of necessity. However, their way of life was in every facet as picturesque, admirable, and socially significant as that of any other ethnic group of human history.

To understand the culture of the early mountaineers, it is first necessary to understand life as it was before the leveling influences of the railroad, the free rural delivery of mail, the mail-order catalog, the automobile, paved highways, radio and television, and dams and the electricity and manmade lakes they produced. This chapter is about that way of life.

No settler anywhere ever put down his roots in greater isolation or more total dependence upon himself and his environment. Divorced from both the influence and the implements of a changing American society outside the ridges that trapped him and his family, he developed this culture of necessity that was fashioned from the rudiments of the Elizabethan heritage most of them brought along from the British Isles. It was a minimal existence based upon what could be found or produced through their own struggles in the mountains.

Although often depicted as crude, ignorant, and indolent, these mountain people adhered to a strict code of personal ethics and civility of conduct. They were skilled in the techniques of survival even if academically unlettered. They were also sensitive to criticisms of their actions and slurs upon their way of life. That sensitivity was real and personal. An insult was simply not tolerated. Calling one a "bastard" or "son of a bitch" was considered in a mountain court to be the first blow, and if one were accused of murdering the one insulting him that way, he was usually acquitted.

The mountain people were aggressive and effective, if often unorthodox, in providing for the basic needs of themselves and their loved ones. Their spartan diets made them lean and sinewy, and their keen minds made them inquisitive and shrewd. They became experts at masking their emotions and remaining stoic in enduring the vicissitudes of their primitive society. They were loyal friends who gave unstintingly of themselves to aid those they knew and trusted, and they were as suspicious of ulterior motives as any wild creature pursuing the goal of self-preservation.

No casual outsider could ever ascertain their true feelings. They could have given lessons to poker players in the concealment of their thoughts. On the other hand, no stranger ever was accorded warmer hospitality than that received by the wayfarer who happened to stop at a mountain cabin.

Those who mistook their childlike directness and innate simplicity for feeble-mindedness were guilty of applying the yardstick of appearances and the values of materialism to a way of life stripped to its most basic fundamentals. It was a life devoid of all the pretensions with which so-called civilized society camouflages its baser instincts.

Here is how Rupert B. Vance put it in his *Human Geography of the South*, written in the 1930s: "proud, sensitive, self-reliant, untaught in the schools, often unchurched, untraveled, he is not unlearned in the ways of the world, and when one chances to leave for the outside world before his personality has become set as the mold of his culture, he is likely to climb far."

Even in the best of times, mountain life was hard and barren of even minimal luxuries. Poverty was a general state, and there were no complaints about the absence of luxuries, or apologies for the minimal parameters of a way of life that alternated between "make do" and "do without."

No one has offered a more carefully considered analysis of the mountaineer and his way of life than Horace Kephart, the St. Louis librarian who lived and worked in the heart of Appalachia for the first three decades of the twentieth century. He described the area as "The Land of Do Without."

Medical care was nonexistent, and nonfatal illnesses and injuries were treated with home remedies or simply borne with fatalistic acceptance of the inherited doctrine of predestination or, in mountain parlance, "what must be will be."

Families were extended, often embracing as many as four generations under one roof, with the able-bodied caring for both the infirm seniors and the helpless juniors. It was a patriarchal existence. The man was the lord of the household; his word was law, but within that context the woman generally ran the household and was consulted about all family matters. Young males had their daily chores and worked in the fields and forests beside their fathers. They would balk, however, when it came to doing woman's work, like washing dishes and milking the cow.

Children had few toys other than rag dolls and "play purties" they made for themselves, but their parents were largely indulgent, allowing them to "frisk" as they wished and to eat and drink anything they wanted, and seldom carried out repeated threats to "w'ar ye out with a hick'ry!" Infant and child mortality was high, and rare was the cabin without an adjacent burial ground populated with tiny graves. Death was an accepted fact of life, and the departed were interred in home-made coffins fashioned from rough planks.

The "hardest of the hard" lots of mountain life was that of the woman of the household. Many were married by the age of fifteen, and nearly all before they were twenty. Birth control was virtually non-existent. Large families were the rule, with seven to ten children considered normal and upwards of twenty not being regarded as unusual. Expectant mothers continued their usual work up to several days before the time of birth and were up at their chores again almost as soon as the delivery was over. Most mountain babies were born with the assistance of only a midwife, whose sanitation was as minimal as her knowledge and whose method was sometimes based upon super-stition, such as placing an ax under the bed to cut the pains in two.

The old saying about a woman's work never being done probably originated in the labors expected of the mountain woman, who not only was a mother to her children, servant to her family, and lover to her husband, but also a household maid and field hand. Her accom-plishments were amazing. North Callahan, in his book *Smoky Mountain Country*, described her daily routine as follows:

> . . . up with the rooster's crow at daybreak, into the kitchen to cook a breakfast of bacon, biscuits, and gravy, in the meantime taking care of what children were awake. A quick washing of the dishes, then a dash to the fields to cultivate or gather the crops. Return at noon to cook and serve a heavy lunch of vegetables, side-meat, and cornbread. In the afternoon, more work in the fields, then back in time to cook the evening meal of ham, vegetables, milk, and home-made jelly. After supper, the mountain wife carried water to the house from the spring, which might be a quarter of a mile away, and then chopped up wood for the fires the next morning. With dark, she washed the dishes again, put the children to bed, sewed or quilted awhile in the chimney corner, then rested her weary self in bed. On special days, such as Saturdays and Sundays, she picked fruit from the trees, went in search of wild berries, canned or dried fruit, and maybe managed to work in a quick visit with the neigh-bor over the hill.

It was no wonder, therefore, that mountain women by the age of thirty were often worn and faded in looks and prematurely bent in form. But they were uncomplaining about the demands of their way of life, and visitors to the mountains often commented upon the sad but singularly sweet qualities of their musically pitched, low-toned voices.

Their appearance of being old before their time was not helped by the scant and somber wardrobe, which usually consisted of a sunbonnet or large, floppy straw hat with a dress made from linsey-woolsey, a flax framework filled in with wool. Later they wore calico or gingham. The one vice in which many of them indulged was the dipping of snuff, when it was available, or the smoking of pipes by a few of the more elderly women.

Weddings often were not celebrated at church but at the home of the bride, where they were jolly and boisterous occasions sometimes stimulated by the indulgence of moonshine whiskey. The difficulty of journeying to the nearest justice of the peace or the inconvenience of the indeterminate wait for the visit of an itinerant preacher often resulted in "taking up" without benefit of clerical or civil sanctions, and little or no stigma was attached to the union or its offspring.

Not from intent but from circumstance, there was a lack of privacy in the one- and two-room mountain cabins. Mountain families understood and recognized the problem of inbreeding, but it was not a deterrent to intermarriage among cousins. The isolation of mountain communities more often than not kept young people from meeting eligible opposites outside the settlements, in which often populations were interrelated from the outset.

The wardrobe of the man of the mountain household was ordinarily varying forms of comfortable, cheap, easily washed, and usually homemade garments he called "overhalls," successors to the animal-skin trousers worn during the earlier days on the mountain frontier. Like the woman's, his clothes were made of linsey-woolsey sewn at home by the women on their carding boards and spinning wheels.

While going barefoot was customary in summer, the tanning of leather using the bark of the chestnut tree and the making of shoes grew to be a substantial home industry throughout the mountains.

Men wore heavy brogans with leather laces, the size and weight of which contributed to the shambling but surefooted stride characteristic of the mountaineer. In winter, the men wore long underwear in which they slept until forced by sanitary reasons to change.

Early on, formal education was minimal to nonexistent. The rudimentary schools sometimes available in the settlements of the region were generally inaccessible by reasons of geography or weather, so anything academic learned by the children was taught by any literate members of the household or by itinerant traders, preachers, and other visitors.

Most adults considered themselves "learned" if they could write their names and read haltingly from the family Bible, and many affixed their names with the customary "X" of those who were illiterate. Children, of course, did receive thorough indoctrination in the practices, procedures, and requirements of taking care of themselves and meeting the everyday needs of survival in a primitive environment. They also learned to take pride in who they were. In 1868, this passage appeared in a North Carolina third grade reader: "A striking feature of mountaineer character is its patriotism, or love of country, nor do we wonder at this considering what a beautiful country they have to love."

Time stood still in more ways than one for the early mountaineers. Few had clocks and thus told time either by means of homemade sundials or, more commonly, by calculating the positions of the sun by day and the stars by night. Months and years were measured in the number of moons.

The weather in general was predicted by the direction and velocity of the wind and the habits and actions of wild birds and animals. They studied the growth of wild plants to guide them in the planting and harvesting of their crops. The possession of an almanac was valued only slightly less than that of the essential squirrel rifle and the revered family Bible. The family that possessed all three plus a skillet and an iron pot considered itself well off indeed.

The citadel and center of life of the early mountain family was its cabin—a rough but sturdy structure built of notched logs with flattened inner and outer faces and chinked with clay from nearby dirt banks. This abode usually started out as one large single room with a sleeping loft for the children, a big stone chimney at one end, and a single "sash" for a window at the other. A narrow front porch usually was added on the front and a seven- or eight-foot lean-to built at the rear for a kitchen.

As the family grew and prospered, a second room of the same dimensions was added, and an open hallway called a "dog trot" connected the two. The building was topped off with a single-gabled roof covered with hand-split oak shingles fastened in place at first with wooden pegs and later by short, square-shaped nails.

Split-logs were used as floors of the earlier cabins and were later replaced by rough planks that were more sightly but less durable. The family was perceived as achieving great prosperity when its members added a second floor to their house with rooms similar to those below.

The best adjective to describe the cabins of any size was picturesque because the roughness of the building materials and the homemade furniture defied uniformity of line or texture. In general, the cabins conformed to their surroundings, and, in the absence of paints or varnishes, the most that could be said for them was that they were "jewels in the rough."

Of the many things the one- and two-room cabins lacked, privacy would have to be placed at the top of the list. Families of as many as seven brothers and an equal number of sisters shared the meager amenities with their parents and often one or more of their grandparents. All of them ate, slept, and performed their ablutions in the presence and sight of the others, often to the embarrassment of visitors who had to do likewise. Most slept in their daytime clothes or underwear, always several to a bed, assuring warmth in winter and varying degrees of body odors in all seasons.

Baths were seldom except in the creeks in summer and when round metal washtubs became common household possessions. One would "burn on one side and freeze on the other," and getting in and out of them in front of the fireplace required contortions that placed more water on the floor than on the bather. The same rough, homemade lye soap used for the laundry was also used for the bath. Early on, outhouses or privies were more the exception than the rule, and calls of nature were answered behind the nearest tree or, if there were one, in the barn. Only the affluent could afford the luxury of a chamberpot or "slop jar."

The jewel of the mountain cabin was its fireplace, which took up most of one end of the structure and served the residents with heat, light, and cooking. A fire was kept burning, if no more than just hot coals ready for stoking, at all times, and the family too poor to own a prized hoard of matches was careful to see that it never went out. If it did, a family member, usually one of the children, was dispatched to the home of the nearest neighbor to "borry some far."

Another unique feature of the mountain home was the ash hopper, a triangular trough cut in a small log, one end of which was raised a few inches, and a frame set on four posts in the ground with its peak in the trough. Ashes from the fireplace or kitchen stove, if the cabin had one, were poured into the hopper, which was kept covered until the woman of the house determined it was soap-making time.

She then poured water over the ashes and collected the resulting lye that trickled through the trough. It was boiled in a big kettle with pieces of fat meat and collected accumulations of kitchen drippings until it formed a soft brown substance that, when dried, was cut into pieces and used as lye soap for laundry, family baths, and the making of hominy.

Kitchen utensils were limited largely to a skillet, a pot, and maybe a Dutch oven. Dishes of any description were seldom found in the early mountain household. Wooden trenchers and dressed boards were used in place of china. Gourds of all sizes and shapes were utilized as substitutes for both cups and glasses as well as for containers of lard, sugar, salt, soap, syrup, molasses, seed, and any other household substances that needed storing.

Every family equipped its spring with a drinking gourd fastened by a leather thong or piece of twine to a nearby bush. Even today, the old-timers swear that no water tastes better than that drunk from a cold mountain spring from a gourd on a hot summer day. Of course, no mountain farm worthy of the name was considered complete without a cluster of gourd birdhouses housing families of martins, swallows, and blackbirds that populated the barnyards of the highlands.

However destitute mountain people might be, they never were subject or given to self-pity. No one heard of a mountain beggar, and the first and last word on the subject of handouts or charity was, "We-un's ain't that hard pushed yit."

Although their demeanor was stolid and their countenances solemn, they liked fun along with their plain, strict, hard family lives. Social occasions were usually mixed with giving neighbors helping hands at ground clearings, house and barn raisings, corn shuckings, hog and cattle roundups, and tobacco curings. Sometimes "frolics" were held, enlivened with generous indulgences in hard cider and corn whiskey. The festivities sometimes lasted well into the early morning hours.

Summer camp meetings were held when itinerant preachers were present to conduct them, and Christmas and New Year's were the only observed holidays. In the beginning there were no Christmas trees, and Santa Claus was unheard of. Gifts to children generally included a rag doll or a yo-yo. Everyone enjoyed a family meal at Christmas, and the menfolk would fire their rifles in the air on New Year's Eve. The standard meal for the first day of the year was hog jowl and black-eyed peas. Hog jowl because hogs rooted forward and "that's where one needed to look on this day," the old-timer would explain, and then add, "not chicken: they scratch backward."

In later years, when times became less strenuous, events like candy pullings, box suppers, and square dances became popular. Virtually every mountain cabin had some kind of crude, homemade musical instrument, which was often played around the fireplace in winter or on the porch in summer for the enjoyment of the adults who would sing along or the children who would buck dance.

Nowhere is more mountain ingenuity found than in the many home remedies for various ailments. They probably developed because there was always a scarcity of medical doctors in the mountains, and, too, mountaineers usually were suspicious of medical treatment and fearful of hospitals. The lack of medical facilities or lack of personal gumption resulted in the development of many remedies handed down from generation to generation just as dialect and political affiliations have been. Household items and natural products often were used for medicinal purposes. Things like turpentine, kerosene, oil, flour, soot, lard, sugar, salt, whiskey, honey, onions, and potatoes were common ingredients of mountain treatments.

A mixture of lard and chimney soot was used to stop bleeding. Lard and flour were used for burns, as was salty water. Another remedy was to place small pieces of raw potato on the burned spots. Salt fat pork was used to "draw" boils and infections to a head for lancing.

No ailments brought forth as many different concoctions as did colds and the "croup." Poultices of fried onions applied with an outing cloth were common. Some used wool soaked in kerosene, turpentine, and/or lard. Mountaineers "cured" colds with several remedies: a tablespoon of whiskey and onions, a tablespoon of burned whiskey, a mixture of vinegar and honey, tea made of pine needles or red pepper or sauerkraut juice.

Asthma was a common malady relieved by inhaling salty water through the nose. Carrying a buckeye would ward off rheumatism, and to insure against ever having a headache, one would place clippings of his hair under a rock.

For earache, there were numerous remedies, such as holding one's head close to the fire or a lamp, or putting drops of castor oil or small solutions of salty water in the ear. Another was using machine oil and a few drops of wine.

"Baby mouth" or "thrush" was an infection of the mouth or throat of a nursing infant. Usually someone in the village would have a reputation of being able to cure this by breathing into the infant's mouth. There were other remedies for this common condition. One was to give the baby a drink of spring water out of a stranger's hat. Another was to pass the baby backwards through a white mule's collar. Still another was to stick a duck's bill in the baby's mouth. An old remedy for a "fretful" child was catnip tea.

Nearly every mountain child was stung frequently by bees, wasps, hornets, yellow jackets, or "pack saddlers" and given relief by ointments made of tobacco juice or snuff. "Chiggers" could be relieved by putting a butter-and-salt application on them. For poison ivy, baking soda and water, green tomato juice, or buttermilk relieved the itching.

Nothing brought out as many recommendations for home remedies as getting rid of warts, which, naturally, everyone "knew" were the result of playing with toad frogs. A few included tying a hair from the tail of a horse around the wart, putting blood from the wart on a grain of corn and feeding it to a chicken, wiping a stolen dishrag on the warts, and putting a small stone in a paper bag and putting the bag in a fork in the road. Another remedy was to stick the hand with the wart in the bag, tie the bag (with hand removed, of course), and leave it in the road so that the person who came along and opened the bag would get the wart. Some old-timers claimed they could "charm" the wart away by rubbing it and saying a few secret words.

As playing with frogs was certain to give one warts, so playing in mud holes would give one worms. The cure for worms was eating lots of poke sallet.

Not only did the old mountaineers believe in their remedies handed down from generation to generation, but they also believed in doing things "by the signs," especially as it related to the moon. Homemade soap would not set if it were not made in the full of the moon. Shingles would curl if split or nailed down while the moon was growing. The ideal time to place them was when the points of the moon were turned down. Fence posts must be set in the old of the moon when its size was decreasing; otherwise, they would loosen. This also was the time when crops must be harvested or they would rot and not keep well.

The opposite was true for killing hogs. This must be done when the moon's size was increasing or the bacon from that hog would shrink when fried. The ideal time to set hens was three weeks before the full of the moon. A circle around the moon meant rain, and it was bad luck to see a new moon for the first time through the trees.

In addition to the moon, mountaineers observed nature around them for signs of importance. Some would call such beliefs superstitions, and well they may be, but the question remained that if they didn't work with some regularity, why did they endure?

One of the oldest was that one could tell what kind of general weather the year would bring by observing the first twelve days of the year. For example, if it snowed on January 1, most of the month would be snowy; if it rained on the third day, March generally would be rainy.

Actions of birds and animals were significant in the mountains. Nearly everyone has heard of Groundhog Day, February 2, when, if the animal sees his shadow, he returns to his burrow and winter will last another six weeks. Old-timers had a variation on this. They said the real Groundhog Day was February 14, and the resulting winter was forty days, not six weeks. Avid groundhog or "whistle pig" hunters said if one caught a fat animal or one with darker and heavier fur, it was going to be a cold winter.

Blue jays were considered signs of bad luck. It was said that the devil owned these noisy, mean-tempered birds and "that's why they are so full of devilment." When one was seen with a stick or a straw in its mouth, which was often, it was said to be carrying the item to hell.

Another animal read for signs was the house cat. If it lay with its back to the fire, the weather was certain to turn cold. Fire also could tell one certain things about the weather as well as family relations. If the fire "tramped" or made a soft, sputtering sound, snow could be expected soon. If the fire burned brightly and leapt up into the chimney, there would be a family fuss in the near future. Heavy corn shucks, thick bark on trees, and tough apple skins also meant a cold winter. Few insects in the summer were a sure sign that a cold winter was coming. Perhaps some of these things seem strange, but one must remember that mountain people were tied closely to the land and the weather.

They believed many other superstitions. Daisies were picked and the petals pulled one by one to count off "she loves me, she loves me not," until the last petal told what one's girlfriend thought of him. Dandelion thistles were sent flying with a puff of breath to make wishes come true, with the number of thistles remaining on the stem representing the number of years before the wish would be realized.

People spent hours hunting four-leaf clovers for good luck, and, when they found one, they pressed it in the Bible or placed it in their left shoe to assure they would meet the person they were going to marry. An itching nose was a sure sign that company was coming. Unless one kissed the hem of a turned-up dress, she would become an old maid. One should not trade anything if a bird flew up at his feet, and a baby shown his image in a mirror would grow up to be two-faced. If one dropped an eating utensil when setting a table, company was coming. "Knife falls, man calls; fork falls, woman calls; spoon falls, child calls."

The strength and importance of custom in the lives of men has been the subject of observations and writings from the beginning of recorded history. Ovid said, "Nothing is stronger than custom," and Plutarch wrote, "Custom is almost a second nature." Edmund Burke summed it up with the observation that "custom reconciles us to everything." Never were these sayings truer than in the mountains of Southern Appalachia.

One interesting source of income for the mountain family was the gathering and selling of ginseng root, a curious plant native to Appalachia and the Himalayas and prized by Orientals as an aphrodisiac. Mountaineers esteemed it and other wild herbs for medicinal qualities, and one of the duties of the women of mountain households was to gather medicinal roots and herbs such as bloodroot and wild ginger for use in the treating of various mountain ailments.

Ginseng grows on the shady side of the mountain, usually along deep gullies. A stalk with two finger-like pale green leaves and little red berries, its roots were shipped to Hong Kong long before the Revolutionary War. George Washington once wrote of seeing ginseng-loaded packhorses going over the mountains to market. Not only was it used as an aphrodisiac, but it was also considered a good tonic for the elderly, who either chewed the root or made tea from it. To this day it remains a valuable product, and mountaineers still hunt, dig, and sell its gnarled roots. Some have tried to domesticate it and make money that way. Those who trade and traffic in the valuable root can tell the difference, however, and don't pay as much for home-cultivated ginseng.

Of all the pastimes of mountain men, whittling was perhaps the most universal. The adult male would almost rather be caught without a rifle than without his pocketknife. A sharp knife was both an essential tool and a status symbol, and the handiwork of mountain carvers remains one of the foremost examples of artistic talent among the people of our southern mountains. Some attempted to make pottery and weave handicrafts, but most such skills as we know them today were taught to contemporary mountain people by artisans who came to Appalachia with the programs of the New Deal and its successors.

By any judge of history, the Civil War was one of the cruelest ever waged by man. It was particularly so in the Appalachian South. Here it went beyond a civil war; it divided families as no war had ever done before. One of the strongest characteristics of the mountaineer has always been his undying devotion to family, but the war severed those connections for a while. It was a painful time. For some it divided young and old. For others, it divided brother against brother; some called it "The Brother's War." To make the situation even more confusing, some soldiers served on both sides of the conflict.

Perhaps it was expected. Most mountaineers were not slave owners; they never had been and never wanted to be. Their inherent love of freedom made it impossible for them to approve the enslavement of another person.

For years in the southern mountains, the people strongly opposed one person owning another. As early as 1819, Elihu Embree started the first newspaper wholly dedicated to abolishing slavery, *The Manumission Intelligencer,* in Jonesborough, Tennessee. Here, deep in the mountains sandwiched between North Carolina and Kentucky, it was published for forty years before the question came to a head with the election of Abraham Lincoln and long before William Lloyd Garrison became famous as an abolitionist in faraway New England. This does not mean everyone in the area felt the same way.

In 1860, in western North Carolina, then congressman Zeb Vance pleaded against immediate secession, warning his fellow mountaineers of what he called a "fatal step we can never retrace." Later, most state legislators representing mountain counties in the respective states opposed secession. Most telling of all is the fact that in the Appalachian region in the Confederate States of America, 250,000 volunteered for the Union Army.

Part of the legacy was the strong two-party rivalry that later made the mountain area different and unique in the Democratic Party's "Solid South" for many years. It also led to many of the feuds that characterized the area in later years.

The Boswell of Appalachia, Horace Kephart, got it right in his often-reprinted book, *Our Southern Highlanders*. First published in 1913, it is regarded as the most definitive work on Appalachian people and their culture and way of life before the intrusion of modern American lifestyles and mores. No one, before or since, has so accurately summarized that culture:

> The nature of the mountaineer demands that he have solitude for the unhampered growth of his personality, wing-room for his eagle heart. To the highlander it is a permanent state of mind, sustaining him from cradle to the grave. To enjoy freedom and air and elbow-room, he cheerfully puts aside all that society can offer and . . . bears adversity with a calm and steadfast soul. To be free, unbeholden, lord of himself and his surroundings—that is the wine of life to the mountaineer . . . .
>
> They constitute a distinct people. Not only are they all closely akin in blood, in speech, in ideas, in manners, in ways of living, but their needs, their problems are identical. There is no other ethnic group in America so unmixed and so segregated from all others as these mountaineers. And the strange thing is they do not know it. Their isolation is so complete that they have no race consciousness at all. There is no other people on the face of the earth to which they may be likened.

For all persons interested in cultural preservation, Kephart's book should be required reading. One cannot read it without being impressed by the worth, color, and historical significance of the way those early settlers lived in the land of the log cabin with their fierce, unbridled, in-your-face reckless independence, the linsey-woolsey frock, corn liquor, old-time religion, that peculiar dialect, and their sometimes mournful, sometimes toe-tapping mountain music.

CHAPTER 5

Making 'Shine

It is not an overstatement to say that corn whiskey was to the rugged mountaineers of Southern Appalachia what cotton was to the genteel planters of the Deep South. This cash crop sustained both groups' cherished way of life. Neither had qualms about the moral aspects of their business. The former was an outlaw, and the latter was a slaver. Both valued and protected by whatever means necessary what they regarded as their special, God-given right to do what they were doing.

History has judged and dealt with slavery, but the record is far less precise in placing an accurate interpretation upon the role of homemade spirits in the evolution of American culture: a culture that, by the way, has many roots in the mountain heritage. Motion pictures that romanticize, books that sensationalize, and cartoons that caricature mountain people and their ways have obscured so much that more fiction than fact exists in popular perceptions of these hardy pioneers and their descendants.

If there is such a thing as the predestination that was central to the Presbyterian beliefs of the Scots-Irish Ulstermen who constituted the bulk of the original settlers of the Southern Highlands' deepest recesses, then we must say it was preordained that they and the American Indian corn called maize were to have a common destiny. They brought with them a taste for liquor made from distilled grain and the formulas for making it. Both were inherited from generations of forebears. They also brought the copper pot stills for carrying out the process.

These people were deeply imbued with a desire for freedom to own their own land and run their own lives and affairs without outside interference, as well as an intense hatred of excise taxes and especially the men who invaded their homes trying to collect them.

Thus, we could make a strong case that the men and the mountains as well as their stills and the corn of the aboriginal Americans were "matches made in heaven." In fact, from the time of its discovery, Europeans had considered the entire distilling process "a revelation of God." For centuries the Catholic Church and its monasteries jealously guarded the secret of it, and Muslims regarded the consumption of alcohol as "a Christian diversion."

There are many speculations as to how the Protestant Presbyterians came by it, but they are all centered on the patron saint of all Irishmen, Saint Patrick. One version claims he brought the distilling process to Ireland from Egypt where he learned it from alchemists around AD 400. Another says he learned it from his fellow Scot Lowlanders before Irish Celts kidnapped and spirited him away to Northern Ireland at the age of sixteen. Whatever the truth, there is no doubt that both Ireland and Scotland were in the vanguard of the distilling saga; about the only difference is that the Irish spelled whiskey with an "e" and the Scots without one.

It is also equally true that King James I transplanted Scots to Northern Ireland or Ulster to "tame the wild Irish," spread the Protestant faith, and establish a trading economy. There they found the Irish whiskey distilled from barleycorn and called "poteen" (pronounced *put-chen*, which means small pot) superior to their own.

They immediately set about learning everything the Irish masters of distilling could teach them about making liquor. It was the fifth generation of these Scots-Irish or Ulstermen who brought the process to America, where they wrote the latter-day chapters of its history in the isolated coves of our southern mountains.

Many factors contributed to the mass Scots-Irish exodus from Northern Ireland. There was a famine resulting from the blight that destroyed the potato crops, economic depression caused by droughts that killed the flax crops, and British trade restrictions on Irish goods. The overriding reason was the attempt of the Stuart kings, beginning with Charles, to balance the British budget with an excise tax on spirits and other imported goods.

The result was the development of a widespread system of organized smuggling of liquors and other taxed goods from Holland,

France, and Spain into Scotland, Ireland, and England, which reached such proportions that by the early 1800s it was estimated that at least half the whiskey consumed in Britain was illicit.

The smugglers were known as "moonlighters" because they brought in their goods by small boats at night, and the white brandy in which they specialized was called "moonshine." These handed-down terms came with the Ulstermen to America and became the forerunners of our terms "moonshine" and "moonshiners."

The other side of the smuggling coin was the almost total involvement of the citizenry in making whiskey in small stills scattered throughout the misty glens and fens of Ireland and the wildest reaches of the Scottish highlands. Their product was a superior whiskey that brought a premium price because the distiller, not being saddled with paying the high excise taxes imposed on the Parliament-licensed whiskey producer, could give attention to quality over quantity.

It is estimated that 250,000 to 400,000 Ulstermen poured into America in five waves of a great immigration that began in 1717 and extended through the signing of the Declaration of Independence in 1776. They came largely to Quaker William Penn's welcoming colony of Pennsylvania, which they chose because of its religious tolerance and democratic ideals. Then they proceeded by Conestoga wagon, packhorses, and often on foot with backpacks to the formidable Allegheny boundaries of southwestern Pennsylvania. They swung in an arc to the southwest through Virginia's Shenandoah Valley and down the Great Blue Ridge by way of the Indian's Old Warriors Trail, which became known as the Great Philadelphia Wagon Road. Into the mountain wilds of North and South Carolina, eastern Tennessee, and northern Georgia they poured. Others crossed the Cumberland Gap into Kentucky. It was one of the greatest movements of people in American history, with Ulstermen hopscotching over fellow Ulstermen in search of the dreamed-of spots where they could shake off the tyrannies of past centuries and be truly free men on their own terms.

The seaboard colonists were relieved to have these fierce individualists as buffers against the increasingly hostile Indians. These determined newcomers settled the lands at the expense of many

Indian lives, and this was the main reason most of the Indians were British allies in the Revolutionary War.

Most of the Scots-Irish brought along their small pot stills and copper worms, which they transported slung under their ark-like wagons, tied to their packhorses, or even strapped onto their own backs. Virtually all of them brought knowledge of how to build a distilling rig from materials at hand, and they also found there were a number of artisans among the Germans of Pennsylvania (from whom they also obtained their famed and deadly accurate long "squirrel" rifles) who would fashion the needed apparatus to exact specification. Thus, it was inevitable that distilled spirits became a fundamental part of the mountain way of life from the beginning.

By the mid-1700s, columns of blue smoke poured from hundreds of stills over the 600-mile stretch of the Appalachian Chain, giving rise to the saying, "Where there's smoke, there's bound to be whiskey." A transformation was thus set into motion that not only changed the drinking habits of the American continent but also influenced the spectrum of emotions aroused for and against alcohol, which affects American life to this day.

As pointed out in a chapter to follow on mountain food, the Scots-Irish farmer quickly learned that the only grain produced in sufficient quantities for sustenance within the constraints of limited technology and the rugged mountain landscape was the hardy Indian corn called maize. He embraced it with enthusiasm, making it both food for his table and raw material for his still. It filled the bellies of himself and his family and, through his still, provided the family with medicine, him with recreation, and his household with a commercial commodity that he could sell or barter for the goods he could not produce himself: gunpowder, nails, needles, sugar, salt, and cloth.

Because there were no roads into the back reaches of the great mountain vastness that was his home, there was no easy way the mountaineer could get his bulk grain to the markets of the seaboard. Inclined by tradition and temperament to the distilling arts, he was therefore forced to take up what was known as "whiskey farming" for his survival.

By converting his corn and rye into spirits, he could transport the equivalent of twenty-four bushels of corn by simply converting it into alcohol. He quickly learned that there was a ready market for his product among his more civilized counterparts in the coastal settlements. They had become disillusioned with rum as their spirit of choice because of the oppressive restrictions and taxation imposed upon it by the hated Sugar and Molasses acts of the British Parliament.

When the frontiersmen of the mountains made their crucial contribution to American independence with their acclaimed victory over the British Tories at the Battle of King's Mountain in South Carolina, they were happy and content in their spartan way of life. But then, the new American Republic, under the prodding of Secretary of the Treasury Alexander Hamilton and with the acquiescence of President George Washington, sought to impose an excise or sales tax upon the manufacture of beverage alcohol.

This act rekindled the still-smoldering hatred of the "excise" and revived the black memories of the searches, seizures, harassment, and injustices suffered in its name that the refugees from Ulster brought with them to America. All this touched off the brief but volatile whiskey rebellion of 1791, in which a mob of 5,000 armed mountain men threatened to sack the town of Pittsburgh. Immediately, President George Washington called out and personally inspected 15,000 militia to put down the uprising.

While the United States survived this first test of its sovereignty, the cost to the National Treasury was put at $1,500,000, a figure greater than the revenue produced by the tax, and President Washington bowed to public opinion by pardoning the leaders. In this controversy, Thomas Jefferson, who called it the "infernal" revenue tax, sided with the mountaineers and had the levy repealed when he became president less than six years later. Except as an emergency measure to finance the War of 1812, the excise was not imposed again until it was levied once more in 1862 to help pay for the Civil War.

The industry did not miss a run during the Civil War, and neither the Union nor the Confederacy achieved any great success in regulating or taxing it. Georgia governor Joseph E. Brown, by both proclamation and reinforcing the law enacted by the General

Assembly, tried to prohibit the use of corn or other food products for distillation, but failed to put a halt to whiskey-making in Georgia.

The new Federal Commissioner of Internal Revenue, when he took office and started trying to enforce the national revenue laws in 1877, was stunned to find there were at least 3,000 stills producing up to 50 gallons per day each in operation in the states comprising the southern mountains.

At that point, the history the Scots-Irish brought with them began to repeat itself in America. Whiskey making, literally and figuratively, went underground in the mountains, and the federal agents sent to collect the taxes found the people not only uncooperative but openly hostile.

The mountaineers relocated their stills into the wildest and most inaccessible reaches of the mountain coves and defended them with their sharpshooting against all invaders, official or otherwise. They called themselves "blockaders" and their product "blockade whiskey," and to the public outside the mountains they were know as "moonshiners" and their output "moonshine."

The post-Civil War, pre-Prohibition "blockader," as a rule, was a man who had supported the cause of the Union and was deeply hurt that the government did not reciprocate his loyalty. He cherished his freedom and believed fervently in his right to exercise it as he saw fit, including the distillation of spirits for his own use and to pay for the necessities of his life. Accordingly, he had no qualms of conscience about locating his operations in a site so remote and hidden that even he and his associates had to strain to reach it.

The still was usually along some little side branch running through a gully so choked with laurel, briars, and rhododendron that the only approach was by worming and crawling with great difficulty through the underbrush. It consisted of a low, crude stillhouse, which was more nearly a shed or lean-to built of logs hewn on the spot and screened by the undergrowth of a felled hemlock tree, and a nearby thatched "nest" from which the "blockaders" and/or one of his two or three partners could watch and crawl at intervals to feed the low fire heating the still pot.

These "moonshiners" could have written a textbook worthy of the modern-day Rangers on camouflage; so well did they hide their operation that an unwary stranger could have passed within several yards of it without detecting its presence. Any federal agent approached it at his own peril!

The process of distillation was simple, essentially the same one the English invaders found the Irish using as far back as 1170. The fermented or "sour" mash made from ground-sprouted corn and rye was heated to 176 degrees Fahrenheit in a pot still of at least 30 gallons capacity. The pot still was a copper container shaped much like a large teakettle with a round lid and an extra long spout to which was attached the condenser or "worm": a coiled copper tube that was placed in a "jacket" or "cooler barrel" filled with cool water or placed in an adjacent stream or under a waterfall.

At the required temperature, the alcohol in the mash vaporized, rose through the cooled coil, and condensed back into alcohol. The first run, called "singlings," was full of impurities and was put through a second run, called "doublings," to obtain the finished "moonshine" product. Prohibition-era stills became larger and more technologically advanced, but the distilling process was the same, regardless of the variations in formula and steps of production.

Other than his "pot" and "worm," the "blockade" whiskey maker had no technology other than his own instinct and knowledge gained through experience. Without thermometers or any other scientific instruments or advanced machinery, the man who took pride in his product turned out corn whiskey of unquestioned quality and demonstrable potency in the range of 120 proof.

The maker and the making of corn whiskey underwent a tragic degradation with the onset of Prohibition. Beginning in Georgia in 1907; Alabama, Mississippi, and North Carolina in 1908; Tennessee in 1909; Virginia in 1914; West Virginia in 1917; and throughout the remainder of the nation when the enforcement of the Volstead Act became effective on January 17, 1920, the manufacture, sale, and consumption of alcoholic beverages became a criminal offense. This turned many mountain distillers from skilled craftsmen of character and pride in their product into greedy, calloused entrepreneurs. Rather than creation of a product steeped in tradition, the process became a ruthless racket motivated by pursuit of the fast buck regardless of the consequences to society and individual citizens.

While it is true that many of the old-timers who revered the heritage brought to the mountains by their European forebears continued to tend small pot stills and serve established customers, they were overwhelmed and pushed out by a younger generation and thousands of outsiders who were concerned only with the quick buck they could amass by bootlegging whatever could be passed in the largest quantities and quickest time possible.

The method of distillation was quickened with the introduction of the new technology of the "thumper" keg, which eliminated the time-consuming second distilling step. The "groundhog" still, made of big metal drums welded together, made it possible for the moonshiner to ferment and distill in the same apparatus and turn out 300 gallons of whiskey in a single day's operation by a single still.

Even more revolutionary was the discovery that the substitution of sugar for grain meal in the mash could cut the production period by 75 percent, and that brought about an alliance between the corn sugar producers of the Midwest and the corn liquor distillers of the southern mountains. The former diverted their product into the illegal channels of moonshine production, and the latter put their still operations into high gear.

While the mountain producers had little, if anything, to do with the rum running, speakeasies, and accompanying gang wars that came to pass in the big cities, the result in terms of its effect upon the mountain people was graphically described by Joseph Earl Dabney in his book, *Mountain Spirits*:

> The prohibition period marked the beginning of the decline and fall of corn whiskey as a fine art in Appalachia. It was a tragic period of ignoble acquiescence by a high-spirited, self-reliant people who traditionally had displayed an amazing nobility of spirit and character. . . . Students of the mountain people and their mores are agreed that Prohibition turned many otherwise honestly motivated but ignorant folk into greedy gangsters . . . [and] brought to the mountains more

whiskey-making, less dependence on farming, more drunkenness, and a distortion of the mountain man's traditional philosophy of self-reliance.

This "evil genie" released in our southern mountains by Prohibition was not forced back into its bottle with the ratification of the 21st Amendment. To the contrary, the adoption of "local option" laws forged new alliances between the moonshiners of the hills and the "do-gooders" of the cities, in which the whiskey-makers supported and even subsidized the efforts of the "drys," resulting in the familiar "voting dry and drinking wet."

Coming as it did at the end of Prohibition, the Great Depression further accelerated the decline of Appalachia into the nation's worst economically depressed area and the dependence of its people who were too proud to accept federal welfare doles. So what began as an assertion of independence and a game of hide-and-seek with federal agents before Prohibition evolved into a deadly serious business of organized crime between the makers of contraband liquor in the mountains known as "moonshiners" and the sellers of it in the cities known as "bootleggers." (The term "bootlegger" originated in reference to individuals who violated colonial laws against the sale of intoxicants to Indians by smuggling spirits to the aborigines in flasks concealed in the tops of their boots.)

The third player in this deadly game was the federal and/or state revenue agent or "revernooers" as they were contemptuously called in the mountains. They combed the hills looking for and "bustin' up" the stills of the "moonshiners" and had wild chases with the tanker-car transporters who hauled the mountain spirits to their peddlers in the cities and towns.

Some of the chases were legendary and have been glamorized in stories, movies, and songs, giving rise to the spectacular and dangerous stunt known as the Big Turnaround, which was effective if performed correctly and nearly always fatal if done incorrectly. It involved the transporter, while under chase, throwing his car into a skid, applying the brakes lightly, jerking the steering wheel all the way around, and floorboarding the accelerator. As the car turned around, the driver aimed it straight toward his pursuer, who, to avoid a head-on collision, had to take to the ditch or worse.

By the time the pursuer recovered and got back on the road, the blockade runner was out of sight. These so-called "trippers" of pre- and post-World War II bootleg operations were the forerunners of today's stock car racers, and some had family roots in the transportation of moonshine.

While the practice of "making 'shine" was common throughout our southern mountains during this period, certain communities and areas stood out over others as centers of production. These included Dark Corner in South Carolina, Gum Log and Tobacco Road in Georgia, and Cocke, Wilkes, Franklin, and Dawson counties in the states of Tennessee, North Carolina, Virginia, and Georgia, respectively.

But of all of them, Georgia's Dawson County was the country's undisputed corn whiskey capital, and it existed solely to supply the appetite of the people of Atlanta, which became the nation's number one bootleg whiskey market. It was said there was not a mile along any stream in the area of Dawson and her sister counties of Lumpkin, Gilmer, and Pickens that did not have at least one producing still, and that columns of smoke reminiscent of the signals of the departed Cherokee Indians could be seen rising every morning from every highland cove of that rugged mountain region. More than a million gallons of illegal whiskey a year poured down to Atlanta out of this corner of northeast Georgia, transported mostly in converted 1940 Ford coupes that were the favorite vehicles of the "trippers" along a route dubbed the "Toddy Trail."

Skilled mechanics made small fortunes tuning up and building engines for the whiskey trip cars, and some of the techniques they developed in fashioning and installing high-compression cylinders and dual manifolds and carburetors were the forerunners of those employed by racing car mechanics today.

The trend toward repeal of "local option" prohibition in the counties across Appalachia and the legalization of mixed drinks in the cities turned the focus of bootlegging from the upscale to the ghetto markets in southern cities. The mountain distiller sold his output wholesale to members of the "moonshine mafia" in the metropolitan areas, who, in turn, diluted the product to a low proof of 50 to 60 and gave it a "kick" with additives ranging from petroleum beading oil, paint thinner, laundry bleach, and rubbing alcohol to canned heat, turpentine, wood alcohol, and embalming fluid. The resulting product was said to be "made to sell, not to drink," and was marketed through "shot houses" located throughout the ghetto areas.

There is no count of the numbers of victims who were blinded, suffered brain or liver damage, or were killed by consuming such concoctions. Perhaps the most notorious case was that of the Atlanta bootlegger known as "Fat" Hardy who peddled 77 gallons of supposedly white whiskey made from 54 gallons of methyl alcohol in Atlanta's black community, which resulted in 35 deaths within the week and left an unknown number of victims blinded and paralyzed.

There are few traditional copper-pot mountain distillers left in the business, although one can still find an old-timer who can tell tall tales about it from personal experience. But the day of the mountain moonshiner and his Scots-Irish forebears, like that of the original cowboy of the Old West, seems destined to be remembered in legend, folklore, and the more colorful and fanciful presentation of movies and television, rather than in fact.

It can only be hoped that in so doing, the admirable traits of character and devotion to freedom that produced their ancestors will not be overshadowed by the cartoons of the shiftless "Snuffy Smith" and his jug, and the colorful terms like "white lightnin'," "corn squeezin's," "hooch," "mountain dew," "widow maker," and the like that have been characterized in the exaggerations that also have come with the passage of time.

CHAPTER 6

Mountain Food

It is stylish today to talk and write about food in terms of types of "cuisine," a French word meaning "manner of preparation." Whether known as "cuisine" or "mountain vittles," the closest thing to a truly indigenous American style of food preparation based solely on available domestic ingredients and resources was mountain cooking.

Southern mountain people, living as they did in the total isolation of their coves and ridges, quickly learned that their survival depended upon finding and producing their own food. There were few, if any, accessible centers of trade to which they could turn for imported sustenance. What few stores were available by tortuous journey, usually afoot and sometimes astride, more likely only offered the most rudimentary staples like salt, flour, lard, sugar, and coffee.

Available items could only be purchased with cash money or with valued barter items like ginseng or buckskins. Necessity forced the people into an existence of "make do" and/or "do without," and their unpretentious lifestyles and simple diets were the results.

To understand the origin of mountain cooking, one must first understand the limitations imposed upon food production by the mountain terrain. Only in the fertile valleys, which were far too few to support the masses that moved into the mountains following the founding of the American Republic, could traditional crops and livestock herds be cultivated and raised. Mountain people were limited to what produce they could scratch out of the rocky hillsides and what animals could forage for themselves in the hillside thickets and on the mountain balds.

That limited them to corn as their staple crop and razorback hogs as their principal meat source. Those were supplemented by what cabbage, beans, potatoes, and pumpkins the women could grow in the family garden, what wild game the man of the house could shoot, and what wild fruits, berries, nuts, honey, and other edibles of the forest the entire family could gather during their growing seasons. Accordingly, the diet of Appalachia came to be known in the vernacular of the mountains as "old cornbread and sowbelly."

Many of the farms were perpendicular, often tilled to a 45-degree angle where the corn had to be hoed on one's knees and often propped up with rocks to keep it from falling downhill. Plowing was done with a steer pulling a "bull tongue," a crude instrument best described as "a sharpened stick with a metal rim." Rows were curved to the contours of the land and also to avoid both boulders too large to be moved and stark, dead trunks of virgin chestnut, buckeye, and hemlock trees killed by girdling and left to stand until they rotted and fell. Plantings were principally of corn, with some rye and oats raised along the creeks, and after planting, all cultivation of the corn was done by hoe, usually wielded by the women of the household.

The green corn was eaten by the family as "roast neers" (roasting ears) boiled on the cob or cut and fried or creamed. The dried corn was ground into meal or grits, usually laboriously by hand in an inefficient tub mill, or made into hominy using the technique of the Cherokee Indians of leaching it with the potash of hickory ashes. The green fodder and dried stalks of the corn plants were utilized as animal food.

Hominy was a nourishing staple made from shelled white corn boiled in a pot with a pinch of lye. The corn was boiled until tender and the husks or skin began to separate from the grains. It was then removed from the heat, drained, and rubbed gently with one's hands until all the husks were removed. After being rinsed several times, the cleaned corn was put in a pot of cold water with about two tablespoons of soda, where it stood overnight. After one more rinse, it was ready to eat or add to soup.

Each farmer raised a yearly litter of razorbacks, which were released, upon being weaned and branded by ear notches, to "root hog or die" in the woods during the spring, summer, and fall. All the residents of the area joined in a yearly communal hog roundup held as soon as the weather became cold enough to support slaughtering and preservation of the meat, each family identifying its pork by the ear notches. No other source of meat yielded a quicker or cheaper return as no other food animal was able to increase its weight 150-fold through its own foraging in eight months as did the mountain hog.

Everybody kept hogs, and on cold winter days when the temperatures dipped below freezing, they would join together to butcher one or more. The fresh meat that could not be cured in the smokehouse was shared immediately with all the neighbors and relatives.

Hog-killing time was almost a festival occasion in the mountains, and certainly it had many aspects of a ritual with friends, relatives, and neighbors swapping off their services to each other on successive weeks in the early winter to get the job done. While it was not a time for the squeamish or the faint of heart or stomach, it was one of camaraderie and good eating for those not turned off by the gory details of butchery or such unfastidious chores as the rendering of the "chitlins."

Killing, cleaning, and cutting up the hog was an all-day job that began with building fires and boiling water at the freezing first light of dawn and finished with grinding and stuffing the sausage and hanging the dressed meat in the smokehouse at the failing light of dusk.

Once the water was boiling in a half-dozen or so borrowed cast-iron wash pots, half the men would proceed to dispatch the hog while the remainder poured the boiling water into a huge barrel, usually half-buried on a slant in the ground as near as possible to the hog pen. The animal would be fed corn to distract him while the owner dropped him with one well-aimed shot between his eyes from a 22-caliber rifle or pistol, or with a blow to the head from the blunt end of an ax. When he fell, one of the men quickly slashed his throat with a razor-sharp butcher knife so all the blood could run out before it congealed.

When the bleeding was complete, the men manhandled the carcass onto a board or mule-pulled drag and pulled it to the vat where, using a singletree and a block and tackle, they maneuvered it into the boiling water. If the barrel were not large enough to immerse the entire hog, the process was repeated for the other end. Once the scalding was complete, the men lifted the carcass high by the hind legs and commenced scraping it until all the hair was removed and the skin was smooth and shiny white.

While the carcass hung, they disemboweled it, taking great care not to puncture any of the internal organs and thus taint or disflavor the meat. Pans from the kitchen were ready to receive such delicacies as the heart, liver, pancreas or "melt" as some knew it, and for those who relished them, the lungs or "lights." The small intestines were placed in a washtub and carried a distance downwind where they were rended and cleaned, usually by the womenfolk, and prepared to be chitlins or to use as sausage casing.

The empty carcass was then stretched out on a cutting table made of boards suspended across sawhorses, and the "cutting up" began: first the head and then the hams, shoulders or "picnics," belly and sides, ribs, and backbone. When they reached the ribs and backbone, the men removed the tenderloin and one of the watching children took it to the kitchen, where it was fried and served with hot biscuits and milk pan gravy for the traditional "hog-killing day" dinner, as noon meals were called in the mountains. Because it was highly perishable and the community lacked refrigeration, the tenderloin was always consumed on the day of the hog killing.

All pieces were trimmed closely and carefully, and the lean trimmings were piled in pans for sausage and the fat placed in a washtub to be boiled down for lard and cracklins, a job the women usually completed that same afternoon. The hams were rubbed with salt and spices and hung in the smokehouse, as were the shoulders unless they were to be used in the sausage, in which case they were cut into grinding-size chunks of lean. The head, after the brains were removed for serving with eggs at the next day's breakfast, and the feet were saved for use in making "souse meat" or "head cheese" after being boiled to release the gelatin that would hold it together when fashioned into a loaf.

The belly fat and, unless it was to be smoked for bacon, the streak-o-lean of the sides were cut into slabs and salted down for curing in the smokehouse bins. After cleaning and rinsing and re-rinsing the chitlins, the people soaked them in a weak lye solution if they intended to fry and eat them as a mountain delicacy, or they stretched them out and cut them into stuffing lengths if they intended to use them to hold the sausage. The ribs and backbone were cut up and divided among the participants in the "killing" and were destined to be boiled as meals for their families during the coming week.

By that time, it was mid-afternoon. The sausage mill was brought out, and the grinding, seasoning, and stuffing of the meat began. This was where the children came in, as they were pressed into service to turn the handles of the grinders. It was hard, muscle-numbing work, and every now and then some overly weary youngster got careless and caught his finger in the mill.

Usually two kinds of sausage were mixed: extra hot with a lot of pepper for the menfolk and a milder version for the womenfolk. Once stuffed in the casings or chitlins with both ends tied, the sausage was rubbed with salt and spices and also hung in the smokehouse to cure with the hams and bacon. Since they cured faster than the others, they were the first of the cured meat to be available for the table later in the winter. But for those who liked their sausage strong, the last and most dried-out links were by far the best, even if they had to be soaked before they were soft enough for cooking.

Smokehouses had dirt floors with a hole dug in the center in which a fire was built. The dressed hams and sometimes the shoulders, bacon, and sausage would then hang above the fire to smoke. Other meats were preserved by drying, and the pork bellies or "fatback" was packed in salt in big bins or boxes around the sides of the smokehouse. It has been said that the mountaineer utilized everything about the hog but the squeal.

Few who lived above the valleys kept cattle, and those who did turned all but the "milk cow" loose in the grasses of the balds to fend for themselves during the warm months. That meant the families had few dairy products and little butter in those periods.

Few sheep were raised and those only for their wool, and, while every farm had chickens, they ran wild and scratched for a living and, therefore, were both scrawny and poor layers. There was little effort to raise large flocks because it was impossible to protect them from mountain predators, and each family consumed the eggs that were produced.

Cooking was done at the open hearth of each cabin where utensils usually included a frying pan, an iron pot, a coffee pot, a bucket, some gourds, and, if the family was particularly well off, a Dutch oven and a kettle or two. Most families had a barrel for making kraut, a press for making cider and/or vinegar, and a churn for making butter.

Butter churns were usually about three feet tall and nine inches in diameter, made of wood or clay, and looked like large pitchers. The people made butter and buttermilk by taking freshly strained milk and setting it in a warm spot, usually by the fireplace in winter, until the clabber formed. Then the dasher, an X-shaped plunger, was inserted through the small hole in the churn lid and pushed up and down until the butter "came." If the clabber was thin or the weather too cold or too hot, it could take up to an hour or more for the butter to "come." The butter floating on top was dipped from the churn and pressed into a wooden mold for squeezing out the excess liquid and for shaping. What remained was buttermilk, which was poured into jars and put in the well to cool.

Many of the menfolk had the rudimentary parts for setting up a small distilling operation on some secluded branch head to run off a batch of corn spirits for personal consumption and medicinal purposes.

Menus for meals were simple and determined solely by what was available to cook at the time. Cornbread in its various forms was served at least once and often as many as three times a day, and vegetables, green whenever available and dried when not, boiled with fatback or streak-o-lean for seasoning, were often the only entrée.

Whether there was meat on the table depended upon availability and time of year. There was always fresh meat at the time of "hog killing" and whenever the man of the house brought in game. Desserts in the form of pies and cobblers were prepared when ripe fruits and berries, both wild and domesticated, were in season. Biscuits were baked when sufficient flour was on hand and were served with butter, when it was available, and fruit jellies, jams, and butters that were preserved for future use whenever supplies warranted.

In the best of times, the bounty of mountain tables was never more than sufficient, and in the worst, there were periods of famine such as those that Abraham Lincoln described from his boyhood as "pretty pinching." Mountaineers were lean with good reason, and the only obese citizens of the hills were those with glandular conditions, not the result of overeating.

Mountain people ate little, and, although much of what they ate might be frowned upon today because of its cholesterol content, there was never enough of it to put much fat on their bones. It was no accident or whim that many of their settlements bore names like Poverty, Gnaw Bone, Needmore, Pore Folks, Long Hunger, No Pone, or No Fat, but they were names always given in stoical good humor rather than whining self-pity.

Regardless of how little a family might have to feed its members, it never refused shelter and hospitality to a stranger and freely shared its meager rations with the passerby who asked for help or the friend who came calling. Horace Kephart wrote in one of his books about his experience in the early 1900s of seeking food and lodging in the home of a strange family that had barely enough meal for its own supper and breakfast. The host invited him in, went out into the darkness to grind enough corn in a tub mill to serve the guest, and then shared with him a meal of hot cornbread, three or four slices of fried pork, and black unsweetened coffee. Kephart's offer to pay upon departure the next morning was declined with the invitation, "Stay on, stranger; pore folks has a pore way, but you-uns welcome to what we-uns got."

Typical menu items from early Appalachian tables in times of sufficiency include the following:

- Leather britches or breeches (the mountain name for strung dried green beans boiled in the hulls) with streak-o-lean. They were sometimes called "shuck" or "shucky beans." "Kentucky Wonders" were especially good prepared this way.
- Ham hocks boiled with Irish potatoes
- Poke sallet and pepper grass stewed together and flavored with streak-o-lean
- Chicken, wild turkey, squirrel, or rabbit with dumplings
- Cured ham or sausage with red-eye gravy and hominy or grits
- Boiled pork spareribs with cabbage

- Baked groundhog (in spring); raccoon, venison, or bear (in winter); or opossum (anytime) with sweet potatoes
- Fried pork chops with fried green tomatoes
- Fried chicken with stewed fruit or mashed potatoes
- Baked wild turkey with chestnuts
- Hog jowl with black-eyed peas
- Quail boiled with cabbage or fried with gravy and biscuits
- Fried fatback with sawmill gravy and biscuits
- Potato, tomato, or vegetable soup with cornbread
- Cornpone and potlikker

Countless other combinations of available pork, fowl, and game were served with all the variations of corn and cornbreads and the cultivated and native vegetables—beans, cabbage, potatoes, tomatoes, pumpkins, and greens of all kinds, including the wild sallets and cresses.

Necessity and the search for seasonings to give more flavor and greater variety to their plain and simple diets led mountain women to seek and experiment with the edibles that grew wild in the forest. By trial and error, they incorporated the substance and tastes of such native plants as the pokeberry, dandelion, and field cress and trees like the sassafras and persimmon as well as the indigenous mushrooms and herbs. In fact, early spring was referred to as "green-up" time because that was when the women and children, and sometimes even the men, went out to gather wild greens, the two most popular of which were "poke sallet" and field cress or "cressey-greens."

"Poke sallet" is the young leaves of the pokeberry and is similar to turnip greens. The young stems can be fried like okra. The gatherers of it quickly learned that they must pick only the newest and tenderest of the shoots because the mature leaves and little grape-like berries were poisonous. The colloquial term of "pickin' a mess" defies quantitative definition: its meaning falls somewhere in excess of "enough" and short of "too much." The generally accepted translation is "enough for everyone at the table, including any unexpected or uninvited guests, with some left over for later."

Preparation of "poke sallet" necessitated boiling the leaves all day and then frying or sautéing them in a skillet with bacon or ham drippings. It was often seasoned with peppers, and sometimes, when they were available, eggs were stirred into the "mess" as it cooked. It was served with potlikker into which hot cornpone was crumbled.

If there were such a category as exotic mountain food, its list would be headed by the "ramp," a species of wild onion that makes the fragrance of the domestic garlic pale by comparison. It was used both as a vegetable and a seasoning. Entire families would hunt for the odoriferous bulb with its leaves around Easter each year. They were fried with lard, scrambled with eggs, or dried for later use like garlic. Everyone ate them, not in gastronomic delight, but in self-defense because the smell lingered on the breath for days, and one who had not consumed them dared not get downwind of one who had. Yearly Ramp Festivals have become popular occasions in many sections of Appalachia today.

The mountain beverage of choice for mealtime was coffee when it was available and affordable. Tea was less popular and generally less used both because of its scarcity and high cost and, in the early days, antipathy of the Appalachian American for anything British, an attitude stemming from the time of the American Revolution. When neither was available, the mountain people found a satisfactory substitute in tea made from the roots of the sassafras tree, which grows prolifically throughout the mountains.

Once dug and dried, the sassafras roots were placed in a pot or kettle, covered with water, and boiled until the liquid turned a rich red color. When strained, it was sweetened to taste with sugar or honey and drunk either hot or cold. The same roots could be used repeatedly and also had a pleasant candy-like taste when chewed; the flavor later became popular for penny stick candy. Not only was sassafras tea a beverage for the people of the hills; it also was believed to have medicinal value when taken as a spring tonic. There was a lively European trade in sassafras roots for a time until people realized it was not the cure-all it was touted to be.

The fruit of the persimmon tree was another native mountain product put to many uses as a food product and beverage. Hernando

DeSoto, who obviously came at the right season, called them prunes and apparently enjoyed them. A recurring mountain joke is about the fate of outsiders who are tempted to try the fruit while it is still green and before the first frost turns it orange. To eat it before it is ripe is to invite the worst taste imaginable and to give the mouth the sensation of being turned wrong side out, giving rise to the mountain term "wrongsideoutards," which natives pronounce and use as one word. Puckermouth Creek near Cherokee, North Carolina, got its name from an Indian who obviously ate persimmons too soon.

After the women of the mountain learned the season of the persimmon, they began turning it into bread, pies, syrup, jelly, beer, and brandy. They found even more uses for the pumpkin, which, as they learned from the Indians, could be served as bread, pudding, pie, soup, molasses, butter, beer, or whiskey. Pumpkins became a staple of the mountain gardens and tables, and pumpkin pie was an everyday dessert, not reserved for holidays as is the current custom outside the mountains.

The cooks of our southern mountains learned much about mountain foodstuffs and their preparation from the Cherokee Indians. In fact, they probably got the idea for the dumpling from these Native Americans. They also learned the technique of what we call barbecuing. Hernando DeSoto first recorded the Cherokee practice of making an open grill of wooden sticks upon which they placed a strip of buffalo meat and roasted it over a slow fire. DeSoto noted that the practice was called "barbacoa." So, from the Indians the white settlers learned the technique and practice of barbecuing, which pervades all facets of American culinary culture and provokes arguments today among the devotees of the various regional barbecuing techniques and sauces. It is a further fact of history that the herds of swine that DeSoto and his legion drove with them as a ready source of meat were the ancestors of the fabled mountain razorback hog.

Some other dishes and concoctions the mountain people learned from the Cherokees have survived more as culinary curiosities than popular entrées of the regional cuisine. Some of those dishes include yellow jacket soup, fried locusts, knee-deeps, slick-go-downs, lye dumplings, blood pudding, and bean bread. The knee-deeps are skinned, parboiled frogs, and the slick-go-downs are parboiled wild mushrooms served in cornmeal mush. The yellow jacket soup is made by parching a yellow jacket comb, removing and browning the grubs in the oven, and then boiling them in a pot of water with salt and grease added. It is said to be a "tasty dish," but the accuracy of this assessment is a matter to which the author cannot attest.

Cherokee bean bread probably was the first dumpling. It is made of meal beaten from dried corn kernels after they have been parboiled with wood ashes and mixed into a paste with boiled beans and soup. Worked into balls or cakes, the "dumplings" are wrapped in green corn shucks, dropped into a pot of boiling water, and cooked for about an hour.

Appalachian cooks adopted the practice, using flour instead of meal when available, placing the pieces of dough in a pot with meat and boiling them to become "whatever and dumplings." Every mountain grandmother knows how to make dumplings, and she learned from her grandmother who learned from her grandmother who probably learned it from the Cherokee Indians.

In the continuing search to impart more taste to plain ingredients, particularly vegetables, one item that achieved universal usage from mountain cooks was the lowly fatback or salt pork. These slabs of cured pork fat were also known as side meat, middlin' meat, or sowbelly in their more common state, and as streak-o-lean when the fat was interspersed with layers of lean and was thicker than that of its upscale cousin known as bacon.

It became custom for all boiled vegetables to be cooked with chunks of fatback, usually deeply scorched for the maximum release of the pork seasonings. Then the time of cooking in the fireplace or atop the wood-burning stove was extended for hours to assure the fullest melding of the flavors of the cured pork and fresh vegetables. This method was particularly popular for cooking string beans and their dehydrated counterparts—leather britches, butterbeans, black-eyed peas, cabbage and all forms of greens, garden turnips, and "poke sallet." Any mountaineer worthy of the name would scorn vegetables not so cooked as "ain't havin' no taste."

While nutritional purists contend such cooking removes all the nutrients and vitamins from the vegetables, they reckon without the fact that the mountain palate prizes the juices produced by the cooking even more than the items cooked. Those juices or broth are what is known as "potlikker." It is prized beyond measure as a delicacy of mountain fare and often is eaten with crumbled (not sliced) cornpone as the principal entrée of the main mountain meal of the day. Of all the various potlikkers, the most prized is that made from cabbage or turnip greens.

The great North Carolina author and newspaper columnist John Paris once wrote that potlikker should not be served to company but "kept, like the best whiskey, for private consumption." He swore that the best potlikker of all is that made from cabbage flavored with a "ham shoulder and pods of red pepper." He quoted a potlikker connoisseur as saying that "only babies and Yankees" sip it. Rather, he declared, "The only pure way to eat potlikker is to crumble in cornpone and spoon it out, or break off a piece of cornpone and sop up the juice, like dunking doughnuts."

"Sopping" is another of the culinary arts devised and perfected by mountaineers. The dictionary says "sop" means to "drench, to absorb, to soak in." In the mountains, "sopping" always involves a piece of bread and, other than that already described of "sopping" potlikker with cornbread, it is most often done at breakfast with hot biscuits and coffee or butter and sorghum syrup.

Coffee "sopping" requires a deft hand to dunk the biscuit just far enough into the coffee and pop it in the mouth before it totally disintegrates in the coffee cup. "Sopping" butter and syrup also requires precise technique. It is done by taking a helping of butter, covering it well with syrup, and blending it to the consistency of thick cake batter with a fork. Then the biscuit is broken in half and dipped into the mixture. One has mastered this fine art when he can finish his biscuit and syrup and butter at the same time with equal servings on each bite.

Sorghum syrup is another delicacy with mountain origins. Often pronounced "soggum," this syrup is made from sorghum cane, which is smaller, hardier, and better adapted for growing in the mountain coves than sugar cane. The making of the syrup was a fall ritual throughout the hills, and many mountaineers preferred it to sugar or honey as the sweetener for coffee, desserts, and other dishes.

The soil where the cane was planted was important to the resulting quality of syrup. The soil in the mountain bottomlands was peculiarly well suited for it. Planting time was the last two weeks in May so that the harvest would occur in the early fall before the first frost.

"Stripping" the cane was one of the hardest jobs in farming. This was done by pulling the tight, fuzzy leaves, which have sharp edges, from around the joints of the cane stalk and cutting the red seed pods off the top of the stalk. Then the stalks were cut off at the base and taken as quickly as possible to the mill so the juice wouldn't dry out.

There, the stalks were fed into rollers rotated by a horse or mule pulling the operating tongue or lever in a circle. The green juice squeezed out of the cane ran through a burlap bag into a barrel, was strained again, and then put into a kettle or compartmented pan. Dark foam formed on the top of the juice as it began to boil, and this was skimmed off with a long-handled skimmer and thrown away unless some old moonshiner took it to make his liquor sweeter. The juice was cooked for about four hours, and it changed color and thickened as it boiled. Then it was strained, poured out into a large metal container to cool, and afterward "put up" in quart jars or metal syrup buckets. It took about ten gallons of cane juice to make one gallon of syrup.

It was for "sopping" the "soggum" that mountain cooks designed and made into the royalty of homemade breads the "cat-head" biscuit. These are king-sized biscuits prepared by squeezing the dough and shaping it by hand rather than rolling it out on a board and cutting it with a biscuit-cutter, as is the case with the smaller pan or buttermilk biscuits. They are called "cat-heads" because they are "big as a cat's head," a term that sometimes is erroneously used in derision of heavy, lumpy, and hard biscuits. Real "cat-head" biscuits are fluffy in texture and melt in the mouths of the hungry workingmen they are fashioned to fill before the beginning of the day's labors.

No account of Appalachian influence upon American food would be complete without the mention of "cracklin" bread. This is cornbread flavored with the crisp morsels of fried pork fat called "cracklins," which are the residue of the mountain process of lard rendering.

"Half-moon" pies are fried fruit tarts made from apple, peach, or dried fruit filling stuffed into folded circles of thin flour dough. They are so called because their shape resembles that of a half-full moon.

Hoecakes are small, crisp pancakes made from mixing cornmeal with hot water, salt, and bacon drippings. They are fried on an iron skillet, turning to cook both sides. They originally got their name because the early pioneers away in the fields sometimes used their hoe blades to cook them over an open fire. A johnnycake is similar but includes flour, an egg, and sometimes a little sugar, which makes them more like true pancakes.

Many books have been written about the influence of Appalachia upon American food, tastes, and eating habits, but the excellent book, *The Foxfire Book of Appalachian Cookery*, offers a helpful summary in the introduction. Mountain food is compared to mountain quilting, made more savory because it was prepared in community.

> What makes them compelling has to do with the fact that though overall they are rather plain and functional, like good warm quilts, there are, as with quilts, those moments of planned design and exuberance that decorate our lives—times when a meal, like a friendship quilt, is designed to mark an event in some memorable way. These grace notes were made all the more savory years ago because of the tremendous difficulty of obtaining any foods other than staples. Or perhaps it has something to do with the fact that, for many residents of the area, the preparation of food . . . was traditionally a means of engaging everyone's energies around a common task, passing time productively, and cementing friendships permanently.

A Disappearing Dialect

Few subjects have garnered more study and less agreement than that of the language I will call "mountain dialect" for the purposes of this chapter. Webster defines "dialect" as a regional form of speech. The Appalachian dialact has been termed everything from Elizabethan tongue to "hillbilly-speak." More often than not, it has been disparaged and ridiculed as a primitive language produced by ignorance rather than recognized and appreciated as a perfected one primarily rooted in the Anglo-Saxon-Celtic heritage.

Some have sought to equate it with the Creole patois of Louisiana, which is an amalgam of English and French filtered through a Southern drawl. Others have equated it with the English of the contemporary American ghetto, which is a corruption of standard English filtered through the deprivation of slavery, the tongues of various African tribes, and the modern jive or hip-hop slang of the present era.

The truth is that mountain dialect is a unique manner of oral communication that largely, but not completely, stems from the same archaic English in which Geoffrey Chaucer told his ribald tales in the fourteenth century and William Shakespeare penned his classic dramas and love sonnets some 200 years later. Of course, it was then shaped by the experiences of two centuries of isolated and independent existence by largely but not completely Scots-Irish settlers within the confines of a family-oriented society in the most remote and rugged reaches of Southern Appalachia.

It is sad to relate that this mountain dialect, like the epoch described in earlier chapters, is fast going the way of the languages of other ancient civilizations bypassed by time and change. Its death knell was first sounded by the invasion of communication by radio, heightened by the trespass of highways that brought the automobile and of hydroelectric dams that impounded the waters that lured the tourists and summer residents, and climaxed by the leveling saturation of the electronic marvel and intellectual monster that is television.

Shakespeare, who would have felt at home conversing in eighteenth- and nineteenth-century Appalachia, must be regarded as at least the midwife, if not the father, of that manner of speaking. He also would have recognized those dooming forces in the words from *A Midsummer Night's Dream* as "the true beginning of our end."

All mankind is the loser because little in the way of written history survives these admirable, hearty, and hardy original Americans who are without annals except for their ballads and folk tales, which have been handed down by word of mouth. There is no prospect of future archaeologists uncovering some counterpart of the Dead Sea Scrolls to reveal the secrets of the generations of isolation. Even with the many new books and the scores of Ph.D. dissertations piling up on shelves of college libraries across the nation, none can ever fully achieve the dimensions and significance of Appalachian English.

It had its genesis in a classic mother tongue and has been distilled, literally and figuratively, into the oral language of colloquial vernacular. It was entirely a language of spoken thoughts, not something written down. Through it all is the application of the early mountaineer's predominant trait of making simplicity out of complexity.

Of course, the cruel and shallow parodies like the comic strip "Snuffy Smith," the overdrawn stereotypes patterned for ridicule like the television program *Beverly Hillbillies,* and the false portrayal of mountain people as depraved and amoral cretins by writers like James Dickey in his popular novel, *Deliverance,* have done lasting harm in how the mountaineer is portrayed.

This proper recognition of the dialect is a mission made even more important and imperative by the growing chain of studies and dissertations that attempt to reduce mountain dialect to the binary formulas of the computers and to explain it, in the jargon of the campus, from the "perspective of a sociolinguistics" (what a mountaineer would call a "high-falutin'" way of attempting to reach conclusions on the basis of cultural and social bias). In other words, such theses are but the elitist side of the "Snuffy Smith" coin.

Recent studies attempted to debunk the relationship between Elizabethan and Appalachian English and, on the basis of their so-called computer studies, reached the unsupported conclusion that there is no basis for the contention that the latter is a "Scottish-flavored" version of the former, and declared flatly that this old romantic view has not been fully supported.

These "scholars" obviously were more concerned with bytes than facts because that relationship has been documented time and again. Horace Kephart, the expert of mountain experts, long ago identified some 800 dialectal or obsolete words in the mountain vocabulary that originated in Elizabethan phraseology—many of them used in almost exactly the same sense as by Shakespeare, Edmund Spenser, and Christopher Marlowe, who wrote during that period, and some of them going back as far as Chaucer, who wrote in the fourteenth century, and Layamon, who wrote a hundred years before that.

Because mountain dialect is primarily a spoken rather than a written language, one needs to hear it to understand it totally and appreciate it fully. It is excessively clipped and when written requires extensive use of the apostrophe to indicate dropped final consonants and the merging of two or more words into one: for example, "I'm a'comin' d'reck'ly."

Written down, it sometimes looks like gibberish, while to the ear, it makes perfect sense and often is lyrical in the hearing. Studies that concentrate on such technicalities as attempts to regularize irregular verbs and failure to achieve agreement between singular and plural nouns and verbs miss the point of the fact that English of all varieties always has been more complex and devoid of precision than are the more uniform constructions of the Romance languages.

Inasmuch as the mountain dialect was frozen in time for more than two centuries and its development had to occur in the isolation of the mountain microcosm, it is impossible to compare it with modern or standard English, which has evolved much more broadly and rapidly in keeping with the trends and technologies of a rapidly changing world.

Instead, we must evaluate and understand it in the context of the times and environment in which it developed, and in this chapter,

through analysis of the words, phrasing, and construction of mountain speech, I will show that consistent characteristics prove both
historical and cultural grounding in original or archaic English and
merit categorization as Elizabethan in origin, form, and meaning.

There perhaps is no more convincing case in point than "hit," the
best known of all mountain words and that most used by "furriners"
when making fun of mountaineers. Few who laugh know, however,
that " hit" is the Old Anglo-Saxon neuter form of the pronoun "he"
and is but another prominent example of the legacy of ancient culture
inherent in Appalachian English rather than a manifestation of contemporary ignorance.

The mountain preacher who prayed, "Holp us as Thou holped
our fathers," had a classic precedent in Shakespeare's "We were holp
hither" from *The Tempest.* And the mountain boy who declared, "I
clum up that aire ridge," could point to Chaucer as proof of the cor-
rectness of his usage or to Edmund Spenser, who used "clomben."
Richard Lovelace, the English Cavalier poet of the seventeenth century, used the word "wrupt" for wrapped. A similar archaic form
included "ruck" for rake. Shakespeare has Lady Macbeth use "afeared,"
and in *Antony and Cleopatra,* he writes, "make your 'soonest' haste."

There is a preponderant use throughout the Appalachian English
vocabulary of both strong/archaic past tense and now extinct words
from Old English. In the former instance, the mountaineer uses
"brung" for brought, "drug" for dragged, "drunk" for drank, "swum"
for swam, "whup" for whipped, "rench" for rinsed, and so forth.

Continuing along this line are these words, among hundreds of
others:

- "friz" for frozen
- "fit" for fought
- "dast" for dare
- "mizzling" for drizzle
- "mommick" for spoil
- "peart" for well
- "persackly" for exactly
- "job" for jab

- "stob" for stake
- "afore" for before
- "aholt" for hold
- "boughten" for purchased
- "peaked" for ill
- "plunder" for possessions
- "quare" for queer
- "tetchous" for irritable
- "sull" for pout
- "tetched" for deranged
- "teetotally" for completely
- "tuckered out" for exhausted
- "wear out" for whip
- "beatenest" for unusual
- "sorry" for worthless
- "much obliged" for thank you
- "bobbed up again" for reappeared
- "stove-up" for stiff

Also along this line is the word "toddick," which vanished with the absence of the gristmill. Not in the dictionary, it once meant "a small measure" and came from the amount the miller kept as his payment for grinding a "turn" of corn: "turn" because each man's corn was ground in turn depending upon when he arrived at the mill.

The list of Elizabethan terms that are a part of mountain speech is equally exhaustive. A partial list includes these:

- "chaw" for chew
- "drap" for drop
- "pert" for lively
- "tetchy" for sensitive
- "titch" for touch
- "sight" and "power" for much or a lot
- "franzy" for frenzy
- "contrary" for spite
- "betwixt" for between

- "nary" and "airy" for neither and either
- "heap" for many
- "puny" for sickly
- "misery" for pain
- "ill-disposed" for indisposed
- "fetch" for bring
- "sich" or "sech" for such
- "tote" for carry
- "unbeknowst" for without notice or warning
- "nigh onto" or "purt nigh" for almost, nearly, or close

Another common characteristic is the use of regular construction of irregular verbs in the past tense. This would be evident in the use of "throwed" instead of threw, "knowed" instead of knew, "growed" instead of grew, "choosed" instead of chose, "catched" or "kotched" for caught, "seed" for saw, and the like. This has its corollary in application of regular construction to verbs that do not change in tense, notably born. It was common to hear a mountaineer say, "I was borned in April."

Some other major characteristics and examples of them are described below.

• Double past tense of regular verbs or adding an extra "ed" to past tense verbs—"drowneded" instead of drowned, "tosseded" instead of tossed, "yelleded" instead of yelled, etc. This is due largely to the mountain tendency to substitute a "t" or a "d" for the final consonant in a present tense verb ending in double "s" or double "l". Thus, in the mountain vernacular, toss would become "tost" and then be put into the past tense as a regular verb resulting in "tosted," or yell would become "yeld" and then "yelded."

This also applies in the form of changing the standard "d" or "ed" to a "t" in the past tense: e.g., "dast" for dared, "helt" for held, "het" for heated, "kilt" for killed, "ruint" for ruined, "swolt" for swelled, and "turnt" for turned. Of course, there is the classic "et" for ate or eaten, in which the "t" is substituted for the final "e" or "n."

• Use of "done" instead of have in the past perfect tense. "I done done it" instead of "I have done it," "I done wrote it" instead of "I have written it," and "I done said it" are standard mountain constructions.

• Plurals of nouns and verbs with "es" and "ies" instead of "s." This is the most classic reversion to Chaucerian English and is exemplified by "beasties" for beasts, "postes" for posts, "nesties" for nests, "twistes" for twists, "costes" for costs, "folkses" for folks, "dostes" for doses, "ghostes" for ghosts, "restes" for rests, and "tastes" in two syllables instead of tastes in one syllable.

• Double-barrelled pronouns. Perhaps the most universally recognized mountain usage is the adding of suffixes of "uns" and "all" to pronouns: hence, we-uns, us-uns, you-uns, we-all, you-all, them-all.
    A variation of this form is adding the suffix "un" to adjectives describing people and used as nouns, like "young-un" or "He's a tough-un." In this sense, the "un" or "uns" is a corruption of "one" or "ones." (The you-all has its famous counterpart in the "ya'll" more commonly associated with the cotton-growing areas of the flatlands.)

• Use of double and multiple negatives: "That boy ain't never knowed nothin' about nothin' nohow"; "I ain't never seed no men-folks do no kind of washin' nowhere"; "I ain't never gon' do nothin' like that nohow, noway, noplace, notime"; and "I ain't never seed no sech thing, nohow."

• Use of final "n" instead of "s" on possessive pronouns. Another well-known mountain construction is the use of his'n, her'n, our'n, your'n, instead of his, hers, ours, and yours. The origin of this form is as obscure as its usage was prevalent.

• Use of nouns and adjectives as verbs. Some examples include "that deer'll meat me for a month," "The moon fulls tonight," "I cooned up a tree," "It pleasured him a lot to go," "I'm surely proud to see you," "Them boys rocked my house," "Ye can't task a man that way," "She wore that young-un plumb out," ad infinitum.

• Use of double nouns. The terms biscuit-bread, ham-meat, tooth-dentist, women-folks, preacher-man, church-house, rifle-gun, hose-pipe, apple-fruit, knock-fight, kid-of-a-boy, eye-ball, shin-bone, and the like were universally preferred to the single noun in the mountains. A woman or man always was referred to as a "widder-woman" or a "widder-man" upon the death of a spouse.

• Use of verbs as adjectives. "She's the talkines' woman" and "He's the workines' man" illustrate the point.

• Original mountain words and terms. Foremost among these is "varmints" for minks, groundhogs, skunks, and other small woods animals, followed closely by "furriners" and "outlanders" for persons residing outside the highlands. They also include "d'reck'ly" for immediately, "tote" for carry, "poke" for bag, "old Ned" for fat pork, "johnny" for outhouse, "sluggin'" for valise or suitcase, "tight-scrooghin'" for difficult, "anti-godlin'" for crooked or not straight, "all-overs" for nervousness, "disremembered" for forgot, "bumfuzzled" for confused, and "lit a shuck" for left or departed.

By far the most colorful, picturesque, and least-recognized characteristic of Appalachian English is the large number of picturesquely original words, terms, and expressions distinguished by dramatic hyperbole and graphically descriptive metaphor that have been incorporated into standard, everyday English without the slightest realization of their genesis.

Those who ridicule or belittle the mountain dialect should give thought to its influence upon what they regard as their own speech when they use the following: "fussed at" for criticized, "blessed out" for reprimanded, "in a swivet" for in a hurry, "fixing to" for intending, "aim to " for intend or plan, "get on" for reprimand, "give out" for exhausted, "hog wild" for wildly excited, "obleege" for oblige, "make out like" for pretending, "orten" for ought not, "mess" for difficult situation or a sufficient quantity of something.

Others include these:

- "mind" for supervision
- "misery" for pain
- "motley" for disreputable
- "narrer-minded" for opinionated
- "old man" or "old woman" for spouse
- "own up to" for acknowledge or confess
- "pay no mind" for giving no heed
- "pester" for bother or irritate
- "peter out" for exhausted
- "plumb" for completely
- "powerful" for very
- "pretty" for something of value
- "raise" for rear
- "fracas" for small fight
- "sashay" for strut or dance
- "set into" for begin
- "light into" for verbal or physical assault
- "smidgen" for small amount
- "quile" for coil
- "idy" for idea
- "lamp oil" for kerosene
- "sorry" for poor or worthless
- "stark nekked" for unclothed
- "spark" for court
- "sweet talk" for flattery
- "tacky" for shabby, out of style, or without taste
- "tad" for small amount
- "get rid of" for eliminate, discard, or dismiss
- "streakedy day" for some sunshine, some rain
- "tuckered out" for exhausted
- "turn out" for dismissed
- "up and done it" for immediately
- "twardge" for toward
- "wait on" for serving or courting

- "way off" for distant or remote
- "wish book" for mail order catalog
- "worn out" for tired or exhausted
- "woods' colt" for illegitimate child

Many, many more usages are "purt nigh gone." The same holds true for expressions like the following:

- "Nothin' will do him but . . ."
- "Rode hard and put up wet"
- "Pretty is as pretty does"
- "Sick as a dyin' calf in a hailstorm"
- "Purty as a speckled pup under a red waggin"
- "So thin she has to stand twice to make a shadow"
- "His mouth ain't no prayer book"
- "You can't get blood out of a turnip"
- "Vomit up shoe soles"
- "On the down go"
- "Rough as a cob"
- "Ain't got enough sense to come in out of the rain"
- "If you want to catch the calf, give a nubbin' to the cow"
- "Born tired and raised lazy"
- "Don't pay him nary bit-o'-mind"
- "Get shed of"
- "I'm a fool about . . ." (meaning "I like . . .")
- "That whiskey is so good it would make a preacher lay down his Bible"
- "Plum dumfoundered"
- "Aye God!" (mild expletive)
- "Let's go halvers"
- "Pretty rough kentry"
- "Shore 'nuff"
- "Stay a spell"
- "As long as I've got a biscuit, you've got half"
- "Fine as frog hair"
- "I hear the cackling, but I can't find the nest"

- "Settin's cheaper'n standin'"
- "He's a hard dog to keep under the porch"
- "He's sich a coward, you couldn't melt him down and pour him into a fight"
- "I ain't been in his shoes, so I can't gauge his footsteps"
- "He's just talkin' to hear his head roar"
- "He's sich a liar, he has to git someone else to holler in his hawgs"
- "Busy as grandma with one hoe and two snakes"
- "Bunched up like chickens in a hailstorm"
- "He put a quietus on that"
- "Every man has to skin his own possum"
- "Beauty never made the kettle sing"
- "Fast as a duck on a June bug"
- "Grinning like a mule eating briars"
- "Never get your horse into a place you can't turn around"
- "You got as much chance as a pig in a dog race"
- "I don't know; I'm up against a stump"
- "Skeedaddle out of here!"
- "Mama said, 'I don't want to hear a peep out of you'"
- "Put the hay down where the goats can get to it"
- "He's as low down as a frog in a post hole"
- "She's so sweet you could pour her on a biscuit"
- "You don't get lard unless you boil the hog"
- "Life is root hog, or die"
- "You're using a frying pan for a fly-swatter"
- "Every old hog likes to hear himself grunt"
- "If you can't help, don't hinder"
- "Never make fun of another man's dog or hat"
- "If you want butter, you gotta be willing to churn"
- "Good Lord willin' and the crick don't rise"
- "You're wasting time; you're shuckin' a nubbin'"
- "Sunday-go-to-meeting clothes"
- "As warm as a grandmother's blanket"
- "He's the best shot in all tarnation"
- "I'm plumb tuckered out"
- "Light and hitch and come in"

- "The Lord willing"
- "If the Lord lets me live"
- "Slow as a schoolhouse clock"
- "Getting up in years"
- "He was behind the door when the looks were passed out"
- "Warm as wool"
- "On a downhill drag"
- "He's got the nerve of a broke tooth."
- "Heaven high and hell deep"
- "Ugly as homemade sin"
- "Low as a bunion on a gravedigger's foot"
- "If there's room in the heart, there's room in the home"
- "Hit was tight scrooging back in the old days"
- "The ground was all spewed up"
- "Monstrous great!"
- "Sit down, and take a load off"
- "I'll beat the daylights out of you"
- "Believe you me"
- "He lives down the road a piece"
- "Don't get above yore raisin'"
- "Bright-eyed and bushy-tailed"
- "Can't carry a tune in a paper sack"
- "Got the dry grins"
- "You got his goat"
- "Livin' high on the hog"
- "You know what?"
- "Steeper than a mule's face"
- "He's been on one of them high, lonesome drunks"
- "I need some food that'll stick to my ribs"
- "It's not far: just two whoops and a holler"
- "He's always two jumps ahead of you"
- "Sight for sore eyes"
- "She's like a goose: wakes up in a new world every morning"
- "Why don't you just own up to it?"
- "I'm outta here"
- "I'm going to cut a trail"

- "I'm going to light out of here"
- "Better be broganing down the way"
- "Rock or get out of the chair"
- "When push comes to shove"
- "Burning daylight don't keep you warm"
- "She could make a living on a flat rock"
- "He lives so far back in the hills, he has to look up his chimney to see if his cows are comin' home"
- "Sure as God made little green apples"
- "Weak as dishwater"
- "He's been out galavantin' around"
- "Spare the rod and spoil the child"
- "Pay it no never mind"
- "Plain as day"
- "He took sick"
- "If you're gonna dance, you gotta pay the fiddler"
- "Thicker than fiddlers in hell"
- "He wouldn't say. He just hemmed and hawed"
- "I ain't through. I still got some creeks to cross"
- "It's over. Call in the dogs and pee on the fire"
- "Chompin' at the bit"
- "I'm hoeing on the short rows" ("I'm almost finished")
- "Give me a holler"
- "He had a hand in it"
- "It's goin' to be a rough row to hoe"
- "That wind cuts like a knife"
- "Throw off on"
- "Crooked as a dog's hind leg"
- "Out of the frying pan and into the fire"
- " A wishbone ain't no substitute for a backbone"
- "Give it to me with the bark on"
- "Give it to me with the hair on"
- "Forty-'leven dozen" (many)
- "Ass-backwards"
- "I swar'" ("Well, I declare")
- "All my borned days"

- "Grinning like a possum"
- "Cold as blue blazes"
- "They jumped the broomstick." (got married)
- "Stiff as a board"
- "In the shank of the evening"
- "Limber as a shoestring"
- "Limber as a dishrag"
- "Fat as a butterball"
- "Clean as a hound dog's tooth"
- "She couldn't boil water without scorching it"
- "I got the missed meal colic" (hungry)
- "Got half a mind to"
- "This may not be heaven, but you can see it from here"

Sometimes it is simply how mountaineers wrap their tongues around certain words. The following are only a few examples:

- "atall" for at all
- "batry" for battery
- "'lectricity" for electricity
- "'tween" for between
- "moan back" for come on back
- "sep" for except
- "idjit" for idiot
- "man-aze" for mayonnaise
- "ruint" for ruined
- "ratcheer" for right here
- "druther" for rather
- "tuther" for other
- "pie-anna" for piano
- "hyar" for here
- "spishus" for suspicious
- "this a way" for this way
- "ya-otta" for you ought to
- "trine" for trying to
- "capting" for captain

- "blotch" for blot
- "bruthering" for brethren
- "warnut" for walnut
- "yearth" for earth
- "yaller" for yellow
- "oxens" for oxen
- "guardeen" for guardian
- "guzzle" for gargle

We must evaluate and understand early mountaineer speech in the context that they were the first Americans to fall back on their own resources; their language, customs, character, possessions, knowledge, and tools were isolated with them in the mountains, and all were suspended in time. They were thus insulated from the evolution that commerce and communication with others normally brings. In short, they became an unchanging microcosm of eighteenth-century thought, culture, and mores, and for more than 200 years, the only changes they knew were those of birth and death.

But we must recognize and appreciate that nearly half of these mountaineers possessed the Anglo-Saxon-Celtic qualities that formed the fundamental elements of pioneer American character—love of liberty, hardship, unstinted hospitality, intense family loyalty, innate humor, reckless independence, and trust in God.

If they had one overriding characteristic, it would have to be independence; they developed as extreme, rugged individualists who were born to fight, never closed their doors, had inherent self-respect, were honest and shrewd, knew no grades of society, and had unconscious and unspoiled dignity that was utterly without pretension or hypocrisy.

Yes, they spoke the kind of English that Shakespeare, Marlowe, Spenser, Chaucer, Lovelace, and Layamon spoke before them, to which they added wit, exaggeration, humor, and twist of the tongue that today is purt nigh gone.

CHAPTER 8

Old-time Religion

Alexis de Tocqueville was a twenty-seven-year-old French journalist who came to America in 1831. He never completed his intended assignment—to study our prison system. Instead he wrote, "The religious atmosphere of the country was the first thing that struck me on arrival in the United States."

He traveled widely throughout the country and wrote an 880-page book titled *Democracy in America*. In this masterpiece, which remains in print today, he made many interesting observations. Here is one of the most profound:

> I sought for the greatness and genius of America in her commodious harbors, her ample rivers, and it was not there. I sought for it in the fertile fields and boundless prairies, and it was not there. I sought it in her rich mines and vast world commerce, and it was not there. I sought it in her democratic Congress and her matchless Constitution, and it was not there. Not until I went into the churches of America and heard her pulpits aflame with righteousness did I understand the secret of her genius and power. America is great because she is good, and if America ever ceases to be good, America will cease to be great.

Many of those pulpits "aflame with righteousness" were in our southern mountains, a place where its people loved to hear the "old, old story of Jesus and his love."

Two hundred years later in 1950, the southern mountains, an area always ripe for religion, boasted nearly twice as many churches per 1,000 people as in the country as a whole. But along with its religious disposition and a place "zealous of good works," Appalachia has also offered more diversity than most people realized or would admit.

As they were settled, the southern mountain states were inhabited predominately by the English, Germans, and Scots-Irish. Further north were many settlers of Polish, French, Dutch, German, and Welsh descent. After 1880, a new migration from southern and eastern Europe took place, particularly from Italy and Hungary. On the eve of the Civil War, African Americans made up about 14 percent of the population in all of the Appalachian states.

With this ethnic diversity was also religious diversity. There were the Presbyterians, the Methodists, and the Baptists early on, but it did not take these three groups of independent-minded people long before they began to splinter. As they say in the mountains, they split "ever which way."

This was particularly true of the Baptists. Fairly quickly this group divided into the United Baptists, Separate Baptists, Regular Baptists, and Old Regular Baptists. There were Missionary Baptists and Old Missionary Baptists, who supported missionaries. There were Free Will Baptists, Southern Baptists, and American Baptists, which were once the Northern Baptists. In all, there were fifty or more divisions including the Primitive (Hardshell) Baptists and the Primitive Baptist Universalists, who were sometimes called the "No-Hellers" because they believed in a heaven for everyone.

Both Methodists and Baptists preached a doctrine of salvation available to all. It was a theology of repentance, faith, and regeneration. The Presbyterian's doctrine was one of predestination, grace, and church discipline.

John Wesley, the founder of the Methodist Church, and his brother Charles came to the colony of Georgia in 1736, but neither of them stayed long. It was here that John developed the small group practices that would later so characterize Methodism. He also met the German Moravians, and in 1738 he wrote of his meeting with them at Aldersgate, England, "I felt my heart strangely warmed." It was his "new birth," and soon thereafter he began to form small Methodist societies within the Church of England. This church became a powerful movement for the masses not only in Great Britain but also in the colonies.

The Wesleys traveled the British countryside, preaching four and five times a day wherever they could gather a crowd, including outdoors with "field preaching," which reached people who had never been reached before. Little 5'5" John rode horseback 270,000 miles, more than anyone in history. Methodism was the type of evangelism that was made for the sparsely settled mountains of Appalachia. Soon an almost carbon copy of Wesley himself emerged in the southern states of America.

His name was Bishop Francis Asbury. He was a churchman just as single-minded as his leader in Great Britain, and just as energetic. Soon he was spreading the gospel all over the southern mountains wherever he and his circuit-riding preachers could find a cabin or a settlement. Asbury himself "went over the mountains" nearly sixty times between 1776 and 1815, "seeking out poor souls in the wilds of America and telling them about the joys of heaven and the miseries of hell."

Asbury shared a pulpit with an African-American preacher, spoke to the Dutch who could not understand him, and slept in crowded cabins night after night. He preached to the German Moravians, rode deep into the mountains of North Carolina, went into the Monongahela Valley (later West Virginia) and as far north as Western Pennsylvania. He rode and preached through Kentucky and went into Nashville, Tennessee, where he preached at a camp meeting. He made his way through the Great Smoky Mountains to the little settlement of Asheville. He even traveled through the rugged Cherokee country of North Georgia. As he once put it in his journal, "I rode, I walked, I sweated, I trembled."

Unlike the Baptists, who were and are independent in each of their many churches, the Methodists clung to the old hierarchical way of the Anglican Church. However, in the Appalachian wilderness they were more self-governing in their organization. Although the bishop did have the final authority, it was difficult to get in touch with him. The General Conference, which was held annually, was also involved.

So, in the late 1800s, Methodist churches spread rapidly in Appalachia. They included the African Methodist Episcopal Zion Church, which had started in New York City before the turn of the century. Today it is the second largest Methodist church not only in the Appalachian region but also in the nation. The Primitive Methodist Church was established in 1840 and still has a presence in Appalachia.

It was said that wherever the Scots-Irish went, there was always a core of Presbyterians, a church born from the stern leadership of John Calvin and John Knox. Early on it was the faith probably most closely associated with the mountain region. The Great Awakening (1726–1756) generated division in the church, and then the Second Great Awakening (1787–1804) further divided it. One large, prominent church that resulted was the Cumberland Presbyterian.

Generally speaking, there were two groups of Presbyterians: the "old lights" who were dogma oriented and the "new lights" whose main concern was conversion preaching. These divisions began in 1837 and, during the Civil War, divided North and South until after the war was over.

From all these divisions and sub-denominational splits, certain strong characteristics emerged that defined most of the old-time religion in the mountains. One was that God is omnipotent. God is all-powerful and has absolute power in all things.

Another is the belief that salvation starts with repentance, which is the feeling of God making you ashamed and sorry for what you have done. It is believed that before one can be saved, one first has to acknowledge that he is a sinner and be "born again." When one has been saved, he or she is no longer the same person. They have become creatures of Christ Jesus.

Arguments persisted back then as they still do today. Is one saved by good works or only by God's grace? This argument, the prevailing one in Appalachia, came from Paul's words to the Ephesians: "For by grace are ye saved through faith . . . not by works, lest any man should boast." An example frequently used was the thief beside Jesus on the cross who was saved by grace alone. "Jesus said so," proponents of grace-only salvation would emphasize. If the new "born again" Christian continued "to grow in grace," that is, to live a life of holiness and display the "fruits of the Spirit," he or she was considered to be "sanctified."

Baptism is another distinguishing feature of the old-time religion. The term comes from the Greek word *baptidzeim* meaning "to dip" or "to plunge," and people argued about how many plunges, how deep, and where exactly the act should take place.

In the early days, most Christians agreed with total immersion, "going under for the Lord." They also believed it should take three dips: no fewer, no more, "one each for God the Father, the Son, and the Holy Ghost."

Although this is changing, many believed the baptism should take place in "living waters" in a natural setting, "not fiberglass baptisteries inside the church house," as someone has said. Many Appalachian churches or communities for decades had a special pond or deep place in the creek or river for taking part in this ritual begun by John the Baptist. It didn't matter if sometimes the ice had to be broken or if the individuals wore their best "Sunday-going-to-meeting" clothes; they still went under.

A number of Baptist churches including Regular, Old Regular, Primitive, and Free Will have long practiced the tradition of footwashing. It is usually done as part of the annual Communion service. Taken from John's account, after the Last Supper with his disciples and before his crucifixion, Jesus took a towel, poured water in a basin, and began to wash the disciples' feet. Simon Peter, who later denied him, questioned his Lord and was rebuked with the words, "If I then, your Lord and Master, have washed your feet; ye also ought to wash one another's feet. For I have given you an example, that ye should do as I have done" (John 13:13-15).

In many churches that adhere to the practice, females wash females' feet, and males wash males' feet. But that is not always the case. As one believer described the ritual, "It makes me feel humble."

"Laying on hands" was/is another long-standing mountain characteristic, a practice that sometimes occurred after baptism or always when church elders ordained and accepted a new preacher. Usually they laid their hands first on the head, back, and shoulders of the kneeling individual. Then others joined wherever they could touch the new preacher or the saved one. If members could not get close enough, they would lay hands on someone surrounding the action. In the case of the newly approved preacher, he could begin immediately to preach the gospel, but before he could legally perform a marriage ceremony, he had to register at the courthouse.

In Mark it is written, "They shall speak with new tongues," and Paul mentions it several times in the fourteenth chapter of 1 Corinthians. This is another practice frequently found in Appalachia, chiefly in the Pentecostal or Holiness movement. Sometimes the speaking continues for an hour or more, and at the end the speaker often interprets to the congregation what he or she said.

From the beginning it seems that snakes have fascinated man. And woman, for it was Eve who could not curb the curiosity that doomed her and Adam. Saint Patrick of Ireland was canonized for, among other things, ridding his country of snakes. In the Scripture from Mark, it states, "They shall take up serpents." In 1909, George Hensley, a Tennessee mountain man from Sale City, decided to do just that. Once when he was walking in the mountains, he came across a rattlesnake, picked it up, and was not bitten.

Two years later, Hensley was "called" to preach, and he discovered that he could draw a crowd wherever he went when he would take up one or more poisonous serpents. The Church of God in Cleveland, Tennessee, heard of George, his snakes, and the crowds who came to see him and invited him to speak there. The rest, as they say, is history. The practice spread until, beginning with Kentucky in 1950, states passed laws outlawing the practice. Before Hensley died, he claimed to have been bitten 400 times.

Some attributed this dangerous practice to the old mountaineers' fatalistic attitude: "What will be will be." Certainly that is part of many mountaineers' demeanors, a way of looking at life or death with a calm, passive acceptance of whatever came into their lives.

The old Calvinistic belief that no man will die before his "time" saturated much of the old-time religious thinking in the mountains. It extended to accidents or even the deaths of babies. For many, this kind of fatalism went so far as to include an individual's personal condition: like poverty and health. "What God wants to do, He will do" and "You're either a sheep or a goat" were frequently spoken statements. An old mountain ballad expresses this kind of fatalism about oneself:

Rattlesnake, rattlesnake, what makes your teeth so white?
'Cause I've been in the bottom all my life,
And I ain't done nothin' 'cept bite, bite, bite.
I ain't done nothing but bite.

Yet part of the old-time religion was also taking seriously the Apostle Paul's admonition "to pray without ceasing." In the early days, and still in some places today, a prayer or prayers lasted as long as the sermon in many churches. Often some members were designated to lead the prayer and someone else was designated to end it, with members expected to join in between. This often happened at prayer meetings with no sermon ever given.

In the regular church service, people offered special prayers at certain times. There were "healing prayers" for those who were sick, who had lost a loved one, who had a family problem; individuals prayed for each specifically by name. The half-brother of Jesus writes about this in the book of James, a book that has sometimes been called the Proverbs of the New Testament because of its instruction: "Is any sick among you? Let him call the elders of the church and let them pray over him. . . . And the prayer of faith shall save the sick, and the Lord shall raise him up . . . ."

There were also altar prayers for which members "walked the aisle" and came to the altar at the front of the church, knelt with their hands clasped together or a hand on their forehead, and prayed with the head bowed. Sometimes they prayed aloud, and sometimes several members prayed aloud at the same time. Sometimes instead of "walking the aisle," an elderly or a handicapped person kneeled on the floor where he or she sat.

Personal testimonies were also common to the old-time religion, where the individual stood and emotionally told of his personal relationship with Jesus. Sometimes it was the story of how one's prayers were answered. Often they were powerful in their effect, and other members joined in with words of encouragement. Stories of repentance or how one kept "putting Jesus off until one day . . ." proved riveting in their impact on the congregation. Many began, "I used to . . . ." It was about what God had done for each individual.

Usually testifying or, as some called it, "witnessing" came toward the end of the service and went on until everyone who wished to speak had the opportunity.

In the early twentieth century, especially in the Baptist churches, the Wednesday night prayer meeting was popular. Each week, members gathered for Bible study and prayers. Each church also sponsored summer revivals lasting one or two weeks. They were big events in the settlements, where converting non-Christians to the faith was taken seriously. Someone recorded a count of the "saved" every night of revival.

Churches could and often did discipline their members. A member who did not take care of his family adequately or got drunk in public could be "churched" or expelled from membership. Later, if the member "straightened out," repented, and asked to be forgiven, he could be "taken back in" by the membership.

People died young in the early days. In 1900, the average life expectancy was only forty-seven years. Funerals were frequent, and the people conducted them in a set way. Often the deceased would have made his own casket and told or written down how he wanted the service conducted. Usually, each family had a cemetery plot where they staked out or marked the locations of their graves, possibly long before death. Often the tombstone carried a message like "She did what she could" or an etching of praying hands. In the early days, flat rocks or plain fieldstones were used: a big one at the head and a smaller one at the foot.

Working in shifts, men dug the graves, and it was custom not to complete the digging until the day of the funeral. They would make sure the foot of the grave pointed toward the east and the head toward the west. Placing the face toward the rising sun was important because they believed the rising sun was symbolic of the resurrection and that when Christ returned on Judgment Day, He would come from the east.

There was nearly always a "setting up" with the deceased one's family, and the women prepared food for the group. Often the corpse lay on what was called the "cooling board": planks laid across two sawhorses. The eyelids were closed, and a coin often was placed on each one to weigh it down.

Often more than one preacher conducted the service. Their remarks were usually sermons extolling the life of the deceased but also reminding the living in the audience that one day they too would lie in a casket and answer for their sins. "Are you ready to go?" the preacher always asked.

A funeral was always an emotional experience. The two most frequently used passages of Scripture were the 23rd Psalm and John 14, and it was not uncommon for a service to last three hours.

The casket was nearly always open during the service. At the conclusion of the preacher's final remarks, the family gathered around the open casket for the final viewing, touching or embracing their loved one.

Finally, the pallbearers placed the casket on their shoulders, since usually there were no handles, and carried it to the prepared site. The word "pall" comes from "pallium," which was the Roman soldier's cloak used to cover him if he was found dead on the battlefield.

A death was always a sad event. One of the saddest occurred when Rachel, the wife of Andrew Jackson, died only a few days before they were to leave Nashville, Tennessee, for his swearing in as the first U.S. president to come from the mountain frontier. "Old Hickory," as the mountain people called him, and his wife, Rachel, had endured criticism during the bitter campaign in 1828 because the two had married unaware that Rachel's divorce from her first husband was not finalized. Rachel was buried in the dress she had planned to wear to her husband's inauguration.

Jackson was bitter. He thought his political opponents had hounded his wife to death. After he was sworn in as president and the frontiersman who had worked so hard for him gathered in Washington, they celebrated on the grounds of the White House while Jackson remained upstairs in the family quarters praying, reading the Bible, and gazing at Rachel's portrait in a locket he always kept around his neck.

Sermons at most mountain churches followed an established order. Always using the King James Bible, the pastor read or quoted the texts of the day. Often, the first came from the Old Testament, which then led to its "fulfillment" described in the New Testament. The pastor took each line of the Scripture, carefully interpreted it biblically, and explained how it could be applied to the current, everyday lives of the congregation. The goal was always to lead the sinner to repent, to accept Jesus Christ and be saved, to have a new birth or be "born again."

In the old-time religion, it was believed that preachers should be called to preach, educated or not. It was believed that if God called them, God would prepare them. This thinking carried into the sermon itself. For many, a prepared sermon indicated that the *man* himself was speaking, while an extemporaneous sermon, they felt, gave God the opportunity to speak *through* the preacher. When this happened, the congregation felt that God had truly called that particular man to preach. If this did not happen and the preacher was slow or tongue-tied, then the verdict was that the Lord had not truly called him. Often preachers opened their sermons with the disclaimer, "I never learned how to preach; I never tried to learn how to preach." Some said they just "talked around" waiting for the "revelation."

Once "relevated," they "quickened" their mode of delivery. They felt the Spirit of God moving them and giving them the words. The delivery often became a chanted style, and the cadences rose and fell with the passions of the preacher. Short sentences were rhythmically delivered with an explosion of exhaling or inhaling air at the end of a sentence, "Haah." Some later called it a "suck back" delivery.

It was a melody of the purist nature, almost poetic in expression. Many believed the Lord was speaking through the preacher. At times, the words became almost unintelligible to an unfamiliar ear. It was God-given native eloquence. "Twasn't studied" was how an admiring listener sometimes put it.

Often, many in the congregation also "felt the spirit" and joined in. The women shouted or "praised" and the men embraced each other, sometimes even going up into the pulpit and hugging the preacher as he continued to preach.

Like most old-time religious practices, this one was based strictly on the Bible. Mark 13:11 specifically states, "Take no thought beforehand what ye shall speak, neither also ye premeditate: but what-soever shall be given you in that hour, that speak ye: for it is not ye that speak, but the Holy Ghost." In other words, as mountaineers liked to say, the preacher was just a "willing instrument." Frequently there was no preselected text.

In a way, this applied to many Sunday school classes as well. They did not use study guides or educational materials. "Just the Bible" was enough, they believed, and they emphasized the Old Testament. The New Testament was used mostly to show how the prophecy in the Old Testament came true. "Strong Scripture men" were usually the teachers and were given great respect.

The first Sunday school ever held was in the colony of Georgia in Savannah in 1737 by John Wesley, later the mentor of Francis Asbury, the Methodist itinerant circuit rider who traveled all over Appalachia. It is said that when Asbury arrived in the New World in 1784, there were about ten Methodist preachers, and when he died in 1816, there were more than four thousand. His Methodist Episcopal Church had grown to more than 200,000, many of them in the southern mountains where Asbury had methodically organized networks of cabins and settlements or "circuits," as they came to be called.

Most of these preachers were not paid and made their living another way. Sometimes they were called "tent makers." The church felt that paying him might make the pastor feel he was better than his peers and that, anyway, he was paid by God and not man. In fact, the Old Regular Baptists did not even take up collections or mention tithes. Only when the church needed repairs was money contributed to the church, and then it was not solicited.

"Purt nigh gone" from the old-time religion today is the practice of "hymn lining" or "lined singing." Of Welsh descent, it was used often in the early days when there were no hymnals or songbooks. The song leader, deacon, or elder quickly chanted two lines of a hymn, called "giving out the song," and then the congregation sang it at a much slower pace unaccompanied by any musical instrument. It was a mournful, wailing sound without rhythm. Sometimes when a preacher really "got to going" and/or some in the congregation began to shout, the "precentor" interrupted the sermon and began to line out a hymn, and the congregation joined in on these "old songs of Zion." It was a practice that went back to the Westminster Assembly of Baptists in England in the 1600s.

One of the old songs frequently used went like this:

Oh, fathers, will you meet me
Say, fathers, will you meet me
Say, fathers, will you meet me
On Canaan's happy shore?

By the grace of God I'll meet you
By the grace of God I'll meet you
By the grace of God I'll meet you
On Canaan's happy shore.

The song continued with the people substituting "mothers" for "fathers," then "sisters," "brothers," "neighbors," "Christians," etc.

When John and Charles Wesley came along, a new kind of music came with them. Charles, called "the sweet singer of Methodism," wrote some 6,000 hymns, including "Hark, the Herald Angels Sing" and "Oh, For a Thousand Tongues to Sing." It is said that John, like most preachers always looking for the way to draw larger crowds, once remarked that the devil was using the good tunes for fiddling, and he (John) was going to take these same tunes and fight the devil with them by changing the words.

In the old days, itinerant "singing masters" roamed the mountains just like itinerant preachers. They conducted "Singing Schools" all through the mountains, needing only a hymnal they carried in their saddlebags and the tuning fork they always carried in their breast pockets.

Decoration Day or Homecoming, as some churches combined it, was usually held in warm weather. Sometimes an arbor was placed outside the church. Families were encouraged to come as a group and bring food for a gathering called "dinner on the grounds," which they always ate outside the church since Paul's admonition in 1 Corinthians just before his description of how to conduct the Lord's Supper was not to eat in the church: "Have ye not houses to eat and drink in?" he asked, and "If any man hunger, let him eat at home."

Decoration Day was a clean-up time. Grave plots were decorated with flowers, galax leaves, or some other greenery. Headstones were straightened if needed, and part of the service was devoted to remembering those buried there. One of the strongest characteristics of religion in the mountains has always been the ongoing remembrance of deceased family members: "We'll see them again some day," and "We'll meet them in heaven." These strong beliefs exist to this day.

Not eating in church was not the only biblical mandate that the people took seriously. Another was that a woman should not dress in man's clothing, taken to mean slacks or jeans. Deuteronomy 22:5 reads, "The woman should not wear that which pertaineth unto a man, neither shall a man put on a woman's garment. . . ."

The people took seriously the Apostle Paul's detailed instructions to the churches. In Ephesians 5:22-23 he writes, "Wives, submit yourselves unto your husbands, as unto the Lord. For the husband is the head of the wife, even as Christ is the head of the church. . . ." This was cited as the reason church deacons should only be male.

Another warning from old-time religion was to not judge your fellowman. Paul wrote, "Let us not judge one another," and it was often repeated, "Judge not that ye be not judged." An old mountaineer once explained why he did not judge his fellow man: "I ain't no judge, and there ain't enough of me to be a jury."

Hell was considered a real place in the old-time religion. For most it was a place of torment and everlasting fire, "where the worm dieth not and the fire is not quenched" (Mark 9:44). The devil is real, and angels are also. Heaven is a rest place somewhere in the sky, filled with joy and everlasting peace. Mountain children frequently heard that when they were tempted to do something wrong, they must do as Jesus once did: say loudly and firmly, "Get behind me, Satan!"

Not all mountain people saw hell in this way. Some argued that just being dead was hell: the grave meant hell. Others pointed out that when Jonah was in the whale's belly, he was in hell: "Out of the belly of hell cried I, and thou heardest my voice" (Jonah 2:2). Some of these beliefs are still very much a part of modern religion today, especially among evangelicals.

In the beginning of this chapter, I noted the diversity of the old-time religions in the southern mountains. From the beginning, there were multiple religious bodies, denominations, and churches. But they all had a common understanding of the Christian faith. While many of the old-time ways are vanishing, that common understanding has not. It still remains much as Tennessean Emma Bell Miles wrote more than a hundred years ago (1905) in her insightful book, *The Spirit of the Mountains*:

> In a settlement in our mountains, one may find Missionary Baptists, Hardshell Baptists, Cumberlands, Calvanists, and what not; but at the bottom they are very much the same. Arguments frequently arise and become bitter over questions of immersions, close communion, original sin, and the like; but the principles that control their daily habits of mind, the beliefs that are the mainsprings of thought and action, do not differ so much between man and woman as the preponderance of doctrines would have us suppose.

Perhaps the old saying is true: the more things change, the more they remain the same.

Mountain Music

Whatever one may think of it—and there are few neutral opinions on the subject—the music of Southern Appalachia has probably influenced all aspects of contemporary American culture more than any other single art form. Over the years, it has pervaded every segment of our society from the country club to the honky-tonk to Carnegie Hall. Its citadel has been the Grand Ole Opry of Nashville, Tennessee, which has been broadcast over WSM Radio since 1925.

However much this old-timey music has been synthesized, amplified, orchestrated, and homogenized through the years and the miracles of modern electronics, its roots are firmly grounded in the coves and ridges of the southern mountains. Scots-Irish settlers transplanted and evolved the music there. Its bedrock was the jigs and folk songs of the British Isles that the immigrants brought with them in their heads and hearts and played on the fiddles they numbered among their precious few possessions.

Adventurous mountain men carried it forward into the plaintive ballads of the western prairies as they left their hills to become the fabled cowboys of the American West and the forerunners of the famed singing cowboys of the movies, like Gene Autry, who got started in Kentucky, Roy Rogers, and Tex Ritter.

Bascom Lamar Lundsford was a North Carolina fiddler, banjo picker, singer, lawyer, and collector of folk songs who could perform more than 300 of them from memory; he left more than 3,000 songs, tunes, stories, and square dance calls to the archives of Mars Hill (NC) College in the 1930s.

In 1915, a noted English musicologist named Cecil Sharp came into the Smoky Mountains and wrote that the music was as "tangy as a crab apple and ebullient as hard cider." He noted that in Europe musical composition was confined to a few elite while in the mountains it was "a common practice of all."

Another visitor was an American musical historian, Howard Brockway of Brooklyn, New York, who wrote in the early 1920s, "Here are people who know naught of the advance which has been made in the world outside their mountains . . . but songs are sung today in this region that died out in the old country a century ago."

Much of the early music was filtered through a five-note scale that provided for repetitious (some would say monotonous) and always hauntingly lyrical songs like the traditional classic "Darlin'," which can go on as long as one's imagination carries it:

> Oh, darlin', you can't love but one.
> You can't love but one and have any fun.
> You can't love three and still be true to me.
> You can't love four and love me anymore . . .

And so on, ad infinitum.

It also included the "lined-off," "Sacred Harp," and a capella voice harmonies of the congregations of the Primitive Baptist churches who early on banned musical accompaniments as "instruments of the devil."

Although the guitar—acoustic, steel, and electronic—is the instrument most closely identified with this type of music today, it is a Johnny-come-lately among the instruments that developed it. The guitar was first brought to the highlands by mountain boys who went off to fight in the Spanish-American War in such exotic places as Cuba, Puerto Rico, and the Philippines. Later it was readily available to mountain musicians at affordable prices from the mail-order catalogs or "wish books" of Sears Roebuck and Montgomery Ward.

The mandolin is of Italian origin and is such a recent addition that its popularization can be traced to its introduction by Bill Monroe, who was not a mountain man himself, in the development of his acclaimed and much imitated "bluegrass" style of mountain music in the years of the Great Depression immediately before World War II. In fact, a 1929 photograph of the Grand Ole Opry shows forty-five performers with fiddles, banjos, and several guitars but not a single mandolin.

Cherokee warriors taught the technique of the one-string mouth bow; these Native Americans made music by playing their hunting bows around their campfires. Musical cow and sheep bells, a form elevated to virtuosity by Grandpa Jones and his family, were first employed by musically inclined mountain farmers who could find no other outlet of expression. A similar explanation applies to the promotion of the mountain washboard to rhythm instrument in early country bands.

The fiddle was and is the most universally accepted and treasured instrument of the mountains. Fiddles were found in both the mansions of the wealthy and the one-room, dirt-floored cabins of the mountaineers. Although the more refined nomenclature is "violin," as used by symphony orchestras, the term "fiddle" goes back much farther in time and is found as early as 1205 in one of Chaucer's poems.

Those settlers who were not fortunate enough to have fiddles to bring with them soon made improvised ones, first from gourds and later from old cigar boxes. By the mid-1800s, mountain artisans were making excellent instruments out of such mountain woods as apple, wild cherry, dogwood, bird's-eye maple, blue poplar, and pine. One of the more notable fiddle makers was Evart Acuff, cousin of the great country performer Roy Acuff, from the mountains of Union County, Tennessee.

The fiddle was not considered proper for religious music, and most of the old fiddle tunes reflect the light and frivolous nature of its music, examples being "Sally Goodin'," "Hell Among the Yearlings," "Long Eared Mule," "Soppin' the Gravy," "Devil's Dream," and the great "Bile Them Cabbage Down." The fact that it had greater acceptance and respectability than the banjo is indicated by the large number of fiddling contests that were later held thoughout the region.

In winning seven Georgia Fiddlin' Championships, Fiddlin' John Carson of mountainous Fannin County, Georgia, attained the fame that brought him the distinction of being the first performer to broadcast his music by radio and to record it for the phonograph. He and his daughter Rosa Lee, who was known as Moonshine Kate, were the first stars despite the fact that little of the fame and none of the fortunes produced in the country music industry were ever theirs.

In 1922, when he walked into the "studios" of the brand new radio station WSB started by the *Atlanta Journal,* Carson was fifty-four years old. The champion fiddler had a colorful reputation as a traveling performer who made a living playing and "passing the hat" when he was not working in the cotton mill, painting houses, or making moonshine.

When he announced that he would "like to have a try at the new-fangled contraption," Lambdin Kay obliged him. His only pay being a snort of the engineer's whiskey, Carson performed "Little Old Log Cabin in the Lane." Though no FCC or radio logs were kept at that time, the date generally is fixed at September 9, 1922. Some who disagree with this date insist that it came within the first week of the station's signing on the air on March 16, 1922, but probably it was on Carson's birthday of March 23. They point out that Carson always came back to WSB to perform on his birthdays well into the 1940s.

At any rate, he did it before anyone else, and he returned soon thereafter with Ed Kincaid and Bill Badgett, two of his "cronies" as his early informal band was called, and played "Sally Goodin" and "Alabama Gals." According to the *Atlanta Journal* of September 21, 1922, he came back again with Rosa Lee and his wife Jennie Nora, who was a "straw beater," to do a repeat of "Little Old Log Cabin." That performance brought him invitations to be a guest performer at the WSB radio booth at the Southeastern Fair in October and regularly in the studios thereafter.

The *Journal* reported that Carson's fame spread "to every corner of the United States where WSB is heard." His popularity inspired Polk Brockman, an Atlanta furniture dealer who had been successful in developing and merchandising "race" records for the black market for Okeh Records, to persuade Okeh president Ralph Peer to bring his recording equipment to Atlanta to record Fiddlin' John.

On June 14, 1923, in a vacant building on Nassau Street in Atlanta, Georgia, Carson cut two sides: "Little Old Log Cabin" and "The Old Hen Cackled and the Rooster's Going to Crow." Peer pronounced them "pluperfect awful" but agreed to press five hundred on a blank label for Brockman's personal use.

With Fiddlin' John hawking them from the stage of the next fiddlers' convention, Brockman promptly sold every disc. Peer immediately rushed into a major pressing on the Okeh label and invited Carson to New York to record twelve more sides.

This venture gave Okeh the cream of Carson's repertoire, including the above two and "Billy in the Low Ground," "Sally Goodin," "Fare You Well, Old Joe Clark," "Nancy Rowland," "Kicking Mule," "When You and I Were Young, Maggie," "Casey Jones," "The Farmer Is the Man that Feeds Them All," "You Will Never Miss Your Mother Until She's Gone," "Be Kind to a Man When He Is Down," "Papa's Billy Goat," and "Tom Watson Special." The next year he and Rosa Lee recorded his classic and personal favorite, "Little Mary Phagan," which he wrote in commemoration of the infamous murder-lynching case.

Carson wrote more than one hundred and fifty songs, and his recordings for both Okeh and RCA number more than three hundred. Only nine of those were ever copyrighted because neither John nor Rosa Lee could read music and had to rely on others to transcribe their works, mostly WSB staff pianist Irene Spain, who later said she was embarrassed by some of the "ugly words" of Carson's lyrics.

Carson got into several copyright disputes with Okeh Records, with Gid and Gordon Tanner, and particularly with Irene's stepfather, the blind, hymn-singing preacher Andy Jenkins, when both of them claimed to be the author of the hit ballad "Floyd Collins." Carson sold all his copyrights for a pittance shortly before he died.

From the age of three, Rosa Lee performed with her father, first as a buck dancer and then later as a guitar and banjo player. She adopted the name Moonshine Kate at the suggestion of the record company after she and Fiddlin' John recorded the popular "Corn Liquor Still in Georgia." The youngest of Carson's ten children, she was quiet, shy, and the total opposite of the "brassy wench" she played on stage and in recordings. Of all the talented and shifting performers who made up Carson's bands—first the Cronies and, at the height of his recording popularity, the Virginia Reelers—she was his favorite. He left to her the treasured violin reputedly made by the son of Stradivari, which, at the age of ten, Fiddlin' John had inherited from his father.

Carson and his daughter also apparently started the tradition of country stars endorsing and performing for political personalities. They entertained crowds for Tom Watson in his 1920 U.S. Senate campaign, for Gene Talmadge in all his campaigns, and for Herman Talmadge in his first campaign for governor in 1948. Herman Talmadge rewarded him with a job as elevator operator and the title of Elevator Commissioner in the state capitol, a title he held to his death.

Reports dispute whether Fiddlin' John was paid for each record he sold or was on salary from the record companies with which he worked. Either way he realized little of the wealth he earned for the companies or the promoters of his appearances throughout the United States. He died almost penniless at the age of eighty-one in Atlanta on December 1, 1949.

The Grand Ole Opry was the brainchild of Judge George D. Hay, who founded it as a showcase for the encouragement and preservation of "traditional mountain music in its purest form." It opened on November 28, 1925, and succeeded beyond the wildest dreams of the "Solemn Ole Judge," as Hay was known to Opry fans.

The program got its name when, after a discussion on the air about grand opera by the famous symphonic conductor Walter Damrosch, Hay came on and said, "You've just been on the air with grand opera. Now get down to earth with us in a performance of grand ole opry." Along came the string bands: the "Fruit Jar Drinkers," the "Possum Hunters," and the "Gully Jumpers." The rest is history. From a studio audience of 125, the Opry went to 500, then to two shows, then to the Ryman Auditorium where 5,000 squeezed into 3,700 seats, and then to its lavish home at Opry Land, USA. The Opry spawned the longest continuous and one of the most popular weekly programs in the history of American radio and later became an integral part of both network and syndicated television programming.

While its report card on preserving "traditional mountain music in its purest form" would today get only fair grades, the Opry certainly has launched and sustained the careers of countless country superstars, the names of whom would be far better known on Mainstreet USA than those of the Metropolitan Opera.

It also created a major music industry in the Appalachian city of Nashville, which eclipsed its older and more sophisticated counterparts in New York City and Hollywood. Those performers from the areas of Knoxville, Tennessee, alone constituted a who's who of mountain music: the list including Roy Acuff, Chet Atkins, Dolly Parton, Archie Campbell, Larry McNeely, Carl Smith, Lois Johnson, Jack Greene, Carl and Pearl Butler, Tennessee Ernie Ford, Lester Flatt and Earl Scruggs, Kitty Wells, Johnnie and Jack, Homer and Jethro, and Bill Carlisle, to name only a few. Scratch virtually any other area of Southern Appalachia and you could compile a similarly impressive list.

The earlist superstar produced by the Grand Ole Opry was the incomparable showman and banjo virtuoso Uncle Dave Macon from Smart Station: a dot on the map near McMinnville, Tennessee. He was known as the "Dixie Dewdrop" and acclaimed as the "King of the Hillbillies" long before the great mountain artist Roy Acuff showed up in 1938.

Macon was an extraordinary entertainer whose recordings preserved some of the best banjo picking and old-time singing that the world will ever hear, and his performances probably did more to make the banjo a respectable musical instrument than those of any other musical pioneer.

He not only could play the banjo in traditional mountain style but also, having grown up in show business and been exposed to the various African-American instrumental and singing traditions, had a repertoire that bridged folk, parlor, and gospel songs of the mountain whites to the rhythm, blues, folk, comic, and gospel songs of the blacks of the "flatland" South. In fact, one of his most popular standards was "The Bible's True" about the Scopes Trial in Dayton, Tennessee.

Appalachian music authority Art Rosenbaum of the University of Georgia described Macon's music as "put across with an expansiveness that was a happy expression through his exuberant personality of all the traditions he had assimilated." Uncle Dave sometimes twirled his instrument through the air in the middle of a song or yelled, "Hot dog" or "Glory, hallelujah, damn." As Rosenbaum put it, he made it "easy to feel the joyous drive of his music." He also experimented with unorthodox three-finger picking techniques long before Earl Scruggs developed the incomparable style now associated as the trademark of "bluegrass" music.

The general statement is often made that the banjo is the only musical instrument indigenous to America, but it is more accurate to say that the now famous five-string banjo originated in this country. Research has authenticated the fact that the ancestor of the modern banjo was brought to this country in the form of an instrument made of gourds with horsehair strings by black slaves imported from Africa and the West Indies in the 1600s.

But research also has established that a Blue Ridge Mountain white boy, Joel Walker Sweeney of Appomattox, Virginia, took its concept and applied it to fashion the first five-string banjo. While working with slaves on his family's farm and playing the fiddle with them at their quarters after each day's work, he added a sound box and a fifth string and developed what he called a "banjar" (or "banjer" as it later became known throughout the mountains). Sweeney grew so good at playing it that by 1841, he and his brother developed a minstrel-type act, touring Europe and even playing a command performance before Queen Victoria.

As recounted by Rosenbaum in his book, *Old Time Mountain Banjo*, the perception of mountain banjo music as quaint and old-fashioned is a recent one that parallels the development of the Grand Ole Opry. Prior to the 1920s, Rosenbaum observes, it was "the most far-out music in Appalachia" and was "shunned by the good people because it was associated with the rowdy element." Nowhere is that described as well as in *Folk-songs of the Southern United States,* in which Dr. Josiah H. Combs quotes a charge given to a grand jury by an Appalachian judge:

"Gentlemen, whenever you see a great big overgrown buck sitting at the mouth of some holler, or at the forks of some road, with a big slough hat on, a blue celluloid collar, a celluloid artificial red rose in his coat lapel, a banjo strung across his breast, and a-picking of

'Sourwood Mountain,' fine that man, gentlemen, fine him! For if he hasn't already done something, he's a-goin' to.'

Appalachia produced several distinctive styles of banjo playing, each of which has its ardent aficionados. The oldest and most prevalent, at least before the proliferation of "bluegrass" techniques, is the broad family of down-picking styles known variously as clawhammer, frailing, framming, flyin' hand, knocking, knock-down, drop-thumb, beating, and rapping. (Yes, rapping!) Its highly percussive approach gives songs both rippling and intricate accompaniments and has the versatility of creating driving mountain dance music on the one hand and delicate melody lines that the fiddle cannot duplicate on the other.

The second technique is known as two-finger picking and is associated with antebellum "slavery days" music. This style utilizes the thumb and index finger in alternating leads and is perhaps most closely associated with the music of the nineteenth-century minstrel shows, which had their beginning in Appalachian Virginia.

Both techniques were laid in the shade by the three-finger roll developed by the incomparable Earl Scruggs. A native North Carolinian transplanted to Tennessee, Scruggs came out of World War II to blend his innovative approaches to mountain music with the Kentucky tunes of Bill Monroe and his "Blue Grass Boys" and create the new type of Appalachian music now revered as "bluegrass" in the truest generic sense.

Of the many legends that thread through the fabric of the history of mountain music, the most persistent and least founded is that of the dulcimer (or "dulcimore" in Appalachian English) as a traditional musical instrument of the southern highlands. The truth of the matter, as reported by Rosenbaum, is that "less than 10 percent of mountain people had heard of one until recent years."

The myth about the universality of the instrument stems undoubtedly from the performances of Jean Ritchie, the youngest of fourteen children in a family from the eastern Kentucky village of Viper. She took her dulcimer to New York City in 1946 and became the rage of the Big Apple with her traditional folk singing. In the wake of her phenomenal success and the tremendous interest generated in her instrument, dulcimer makers sprang up everywhere, and the instrument became a staple of the inventory of every mountain crafts shop inside and outside Appalachia.

The origin of the mountain or plucked dulcimer is obscure, but probably it is a descendant of the German "scheitholt" or zither, which the early German settlers of mountainous Western Pennsylvania brought to this country. Examples of it found in Pennsylvania's Mercer Museum show it to be a long, narrow, and straight-sided instrument with the fingerboard made onto its body.

The Southern Appalachian version was more crude, less refined, and more diversified in style and construction. Its fingerboard was almost always raised, and the instrument itself took on a variety of curvaceous shapes. It usually had only three or four strings that one strummed with a turkey quill and chorded with a small stick called a "noter."

Usually played on the lap by females, the dulcimer combined the tone of a wooden instrument with the tune of bagpipes, and its plaintive sound coupled with falsetto female vocals is probably why it captured public imagination as typical of mountain music. In fact, it is not as old as the banjo and probably was less prevalent throughout the mountains than the mouth bow.

What the guitar lacked in tradition in mountain music, it made up for in immediate popularity following its introduction. What Ralph Peer did for country music in general with his recordings of the music of Fiddlin' John Carson, he did specifically for the guitar when he "discovered" and recorded the Carter Family in Bristol, Tennessee, in 1927.

Scott County in western Virginia joins the Tennessee border. Carters had been in this mountain area for more than a century. Carters Fort was built along the Wilderness Road in 1784. Coal mining was not extensive in this area; it was more agricultural, with small family farms.

On the first day of April 1927, Alvin Pleasant Delaney Carter, his wife Sara, and his sister-in-law Maybelle traveled twenty-five miles down to Bristol, Tennessee, on the state line. There they recorded for

Ralph Peer who had placed a notice in the local newspaper advertising that he represented Victor Records and wished to record local musicians.

The result of this first meeting was phenomenal. Over the next twelve years, the Carters recorded more than 273 masters. Thanks to the most powerful radio station in the world—XERA—on the Mexican border, in the 1930s they acquired worldwide popularity, including Australia, India, Canada, Europe, and South Africa.

After their XERA experience, they operated primarily out of Charlotte, North Carolina, and played their music on radio station WBT. In 1943, the trio broke up. A.P. went back home to Scott County, Sara moved to California, and Maybelle, with her daughters, began working out of WRVA of Richmond, Virginia, as Mother Maybelle and the Carter Sisters.

On that day in 1927 as they left to go to Bristol to record for Ralph Peer, Maybelle had to be asked to go back in the house to get her guitar, as she considered herself a singer, not a "picker." This "singer, not a picker" became the innovator of the up-and-down brushing technique of playing and would become the guru of all guitar pickers. With her protégé and Clinch Mountain neighbor, Chet Atkins, the pair probably had more influence upon the evolving style of country music than any other two individuals. No country band could survive today without lead, rhythm, bass guitars, and, as many would contend, steel guitars. Maybelle Carter also pioneered the use of the autoharp, and, while it remained more an acclaimed curiosity than an accepted instrument, she, her daughter June, and "Pop" Stoneman made it almost as mythical a mountain instrument as the dulcimer.

Even with the Carters' popularity, a young Knoxville fiddler who could sing "loud and clear" became the Opry's most distinctive voice. Roy Acuff was born in 1903 in Union County, Tennessee, in the Great Smoky Mountains, the grandson of a Union soldier. When Roy was a teenager, the family moved from Maynardville to Fountain City, just outside Knoxville.

In fall 1936, twelve years after Carson's first radio appearance and eight years after the Carters went to Bristol, Acuff had a noon show on radio station WROC. A Columbia Records scout heard Acuff sing a song: a hymn he called "The Bird."

Acuff found the song a few years earlier and was fascinated with it. The tune was a close variation of "I'm Thinking Today of My Blue Eyes," and a Reverend Gary Smith had put words to it and called it "On the Wings of the Great Speckled Bird."

Roy later added some of his own verses, explaining the "bird" was the Bible and the church and came from Jeremiah 12:9, "Mine heritage is unto me as a speckled bird . . . ."

Based largely on the popularity of this one song and his skill as a fiddler, in 1936 Roy was invited to audition for the Opry and was rejected. At that time, they were not interested in vocalists; they wanted string bands. So Roy organized the "Smokey Mountain Boys" and two years later was accepted. Immediately his vocals and irrepressible showmanship made him the Opry's most popular performer.

This was the same year, 1938, that the Carter family moved to Texas where they broadcast over the 150,000-watt station XERA in Mexico.

In 1943, the signal of the radio station that carried the Opry, WSM, was expanded and, for the first time, could be heard coast to coast. Roy's voice and style became known nationwide. When this happened, Tennessee governor Prentice Cooper remarked that Acuff would "disgrace" Nashville by making it the "hillbilly capital" of the world. Little did the governor realize that Nashville would become world famous as "Music City, USA," and Roy Acuff would become the "King of Country Music" and, in 1948, run unsuccessfully for governor of Tennessee himself.

WSM and the Grand Ole Opry were not the only outlets for mountain music. Beginning in 1933, the Wheeling Jamboree has been broadcast on Radio Station WWVA. Usually broadcast from Wheeling's Capitol Theater, it was the starting place for acts like Grandpa Jones, Wilma Lee and Stoney Cooper, and Hawkshaw Hawkins, all who later became members of the Grand Ole Opry.

WNOX was another early source of mountain music in Knoxville, Tennessee, as early as 1921. From its studios came Pee Wee King, Carl Story, Kitty Wells, comedian Archie Campbell, and many others.

Beginning in the 1940s, WPAQ from Mount Airy, North Carolina, programmed much of the traditional music of the mountains, including Lester Flatt and Earl Scruggs, Mac Wiseman, and The Stanley Brothers, among many others.

Chester Burton Atkins was born in the same Clinch Mountain area as the Carter family. Early on he displayed a natural bent for music and by nine became proficient on the guitar and the fiddle to play at Saturday night hoedowns, roadhouses, and tourist camps.

As a teenager, he got a job with the National Youth Administration and saved his money to buy an electric guitar. When his father left for a war job in Cincinnati and young Atkins was turned down by the draft because of his asthma, he went to Tennessee and landed a performing job on the Archie Campbell/Bill Carlisle Show on radio station WNOX in Knoxville. Three years later he was heard coast-to-coast on another super radio station, WLW in Cincinnati.

In 1950, he joined Mother Maybelle and the Carter Sisters and accompanied them to the Grand Ole Opry. He also began recording sessions with scores of artists, notably Hank Williams and the Carlisles.

When he came to Nashville with RCA, customers were getting tired of fiddle and steel, and country record sales were in a nosedive. That was when Chet came up with what was eventually called the Nashville Sound and started making records with guitars, pianos, horns, vocal choruses, and new instrumental and vocal sounds.

Chet Atkins was either the discoverer and/or molding genius behind the development of such musical superstars as Dolly Parton, Willie Nelson, Waylon Jennings, Floyd Cramer, Jim Reeves, Hank Locklin, Don Gibson, Skeeter Davis, Connie Smith, Dottie West, Jerry Reed, Porter Wagoner, Charley Pride, and George Hamilton IV, to name only a few.

Proving that a country musician can play more than three-chord hillbilly songs, Chet's sophisticated and polished approach brought perfection to the unique finger-picking style of guitar performances initiated by his idol, Merle Travis, in which the melody is played by the fingers or a pick held by the fingers and the accompanying base line is added with the thumb.

Atkins scored successes with Jim Reeves's "Four Walls" and Don Gibson's double-sided smash hits, "Oh, Lonesome Me" and "I Can't Stop Loving You." He mixed flamenco, country, pop, and rock, making his mark and perfecting his new sound by adapting songwriter Don Robertson's approach in bending piano notes like a steel guitar on his demo of "Please Help Me, I'm Falling" and teaching it to Floyd Cramer. Two smash recordings resulted: Hank Locklin's "Falling" and Cramer's "Last Date."

Chet did various RCA pop sessions in Nashville with Perry Como, who was from the mountains of Southwest Pennsylvania, and he performed and recorded with the Boston Pops.

Of all the musicians of Appalachia, none made a greater contribution to giving respectability and popularity to "hillbilly" music than James Gideon "Gid" Tanner, a chicken farmer from Dacula, Georgia. With his wild band of musical geniuses known as the Skillet Lickers, they also built a bridge between traditional mountain music and modern popular music. They not only gave respectability and popularity to what previously had been derided as "hillbilly" music, but also served as the initial catalyst in the sweeping electronic evolution that helped mix country, jazz, blues, and urban pop and give commonality to American music as we know it today.

Had it not been for the lure of the burgeoning music recording and radio broadcasting industries, James Gideon Tanner probably would have been content to limit his musical activities to occasional forays out of his Walton County, Georgia, farm to joust with the likes of Fiddlin' John Carson, his senior, and Clayton McMichen, his junior, in the fiddling competitions of the time.

It was McMichen, called "Pappy," who won the Fiddling Championship of the United States in 1926 and who followed John Carson's appearance on radio station WSB by only a few months. He played the fiddle on Jimmie Rodgers's early recordings, helped Gene Autry in his early career, and discovered Merle Travis as a teenager in the coalmining town of Drakesboro, Kentucky.

Frank Walker of Columbia Records then invited Tanner to come to New York to help that company catch up with Okeh Records' highly successful issues of Carson's country recordings. Gid took with him his blind friend, Riley Puckett, who later gained fame as the first of the crooners and rhythm guitarists. On March 7, 1924, they became the first mountain artists to record for Columbia.

Further, at Walker's request, Tanner came home and assembled the Skillet Lickers, which, with periodic shifts in membership, was to become one of the most highly respected and popular names in the field of string band music. From 1926 until their final disbandment in 1934, they made a phenomenal total of 565 recordings combining hillbilly with popular music, including the forever popular "John Henry" and the classic "Down Yonder," which was one of the first instrumental records to sell a million copies. They also introduced comedy to the recording industry with their rural skits borrowed from the minstrel show format of humorous dialogue interspersed with snatches from previously recorded songs and instrumentals.

At one of these performances in Upper Manhattan in New York City, a struggling Brooklyn cartoonist named Alfred Gerald Caplin and his wife Catherine observed a skit by the Skillet Lickers, and the idea for *Li'l Abner* was born. This handsome, one-gallus "hillbilly" from Dogpatch would first appear in the *New York Daily Mirror* in August 1934. At its height of popularity, Al Capp's cartoon strip appeared in 900 newspapers, reaching 90 million readers a day, and continued for 43 years. So, daily for a generation, this stereotype of persons and place was seared into the senses of America.

Besides Tanner and Puckett, the Skillet Lickers originally included McMichen and his brother-in-law Bert Layne as fiddlers and Fate Norris on the banjo and the harmonica. Layne was replaced by McMichen's brilliant young protégé, Lowe Stokes, from Rome, Georgia, whose contest with Carson for the Fiddlin' Championship was the subject of Stephen Vincent Benet's *The Mountain Whippoorwill.*

Although the original is "purt nigh gone," mountain music left a lasting legacy. Those rugged, talented, and stoic settlers brought their music with them, then shaped it in the course of their struggle to survive and made it an integral part of the total culture of the modern American nation.

CHAPTER 10

Mountain Humor

In a tiny mountain village in a tiny mountain valley, a house caught on fire. With no fire department—not even a volunteer one—the townspeople looked on helplessly as the structure was engulfed in flames.

Suddenly, out of one of the nearby hollows came a local character everyone knew as Fuzz. He drove his battered pickup, one fender off and another barely on. Many of his extended family rode with him, packed into the truck's cab and rear bed.

Instead of stopping where the onlookers stood a safe distance away, he drove his truck and passengers directly into the raging fire. They piled out—at least eight of them—and with old toe sacks, quilts, and pine brushes from the back of the truck, they began sweeping and stomping, and believe it or not, they put the fire out.

The townspeople were dumbfounded and amazed at what they had just witnessed. The town mayor was there and immediately took up a collection from among the still amazed townsfolk. He then called the newly minted hero of the day to come forward.

Fuzz had lost one brogan, his eyebrows were singed off, and an entire sleeve was torn from his shirt.

"Fuzz," the mayor said, "this is the most heroic thing we've ever seen in our little town, and we want to show our appreciation. Here's $8.70 we've took up for you and your family." He paused. "By the way, what are you going to do with it?"

Face black from smoke, somewhat embarrassed with all the attention, Fuzz answered, "Well, the first thing I'm going to do is get some brakes put on that pickup!"

That story demonstrates typical mountain humor, the kind that Appalachian scholar Wilma Dykeman once called "as unique as churning butter." There are thousands of such stories: a few true, most embellished, tall tales that work better heard than read.

The most famous and, perhaps, first such teller of tall tales in the southern mountains was the well-known spinner of yarns, congressman, and finally hero of the Alamo, David Crockett himself.

Over the years, so much exaggeration has distorted Crockett's life that today it is impossible to separate fact from fiction. We know he was born in the Holston River area of North Carolina/Virginia in 1786 of Scots-Irish stock. He left home at age thirteen to help a man herd cattle 250 miles away, then turned around and finally wandered back home over the next three years, stopping to do another long cattle drive and work months at a time in taverns on his way back. This is where the tellers of tall tales first intrigued him. Although David had only six months of schooling, he could write and spell phonetically, which helped capture the color of the stories he began to tell and write about.

Always moving westward into the frontier, staying nowhere for long, Crockett speculated in land and ran for Congress. He lost his first race but captured a following of uneducated men like himself who admired his toughness and found his colorful dialect and way of putting things memorable.

Crockett fought alongside his fellow Tennessean, Andrew Jackson, in the Creek Indian Wars, and in the beginning the two were political allies. Later, he split with Old Hickory over whether there should be a U.S. bank: Jackson opposed it, but Crockett supported it because he felt it would help him and others like him get more money for land speculation. The Jackson-Crockett split also probably had something to do with two big egos inhabiting one state. Over time, their relationship grew bitter, with Crockett calling his enemy "King Andrew" and Jackson referring to Crockett as "Davy" as if he were an adolescent.

Crockett served three terms in Congress but was defeated in several other elections. His widespread fame resulted from a book called *The Lion of the West* about a frontier hero, modeled after Crockett, with the name Nimrod Wildfire. A huge hit, the book was made into a play that widely toured the country. The book and the play made

Crockett's wit and mountain manner nationally famous—so famous, in fact, that Crockett decided to write his own book. He called his autobiography *A Narrative of the Life of David Crockett of the State of Tennessee*. It, too, became a national bestseller. The first printing sold out in three weeks, and it was reprinted more than a dozen times.

Crockett was a colorful character, a quick wit, and a naturally funny man. His quaint speech, phonetic spelling, and interesting life story not only brought him much attention but also, for a short while, made him a potential presidential candidate for the Whig Party to challenge Jackson. Crockett's humor could be crude and bawdy. He was always in debt, and, after being defeated by his homefolks in a bitter reelection campaign, he responded by declaring in his concession speech, "You voters can go to hell. I'm going to Texas."

And he did. The vastness of all that land in the west lured him. He "always had to be going into the sunset," as Daniel Boone put it, and his old friend Sam Houston, also of Tennessee, was already there. Crockett gave a drunken farewell party, played the fiddle, and told a few stories. Then he left with about a half-dozen friends. All along the way, this colorful celebrity was entertained, toasted, and asked to speak, which he gladly did. Some volunteered to go with him when they heard him promise that he "was going to grin all the Mexicans out of Texas."

His group, called the Tennessee Mounted Volunteers, arrived at San Antonio in January 1836. In March, they, along with about 300 others including the famous James Bowie and William Travis, were killed in the historic battle at the Alamo.

A New York paper declared, "No other country but our own ever did or ever will produce a character such as this." After his death, Crockett's autobiography once again became a national best-seller.

A few decades later, Samuel Clemens (Mark Twain) used young David, the wandering, quick-witted teenager, as his model for Huckleberry Finn.

Once when Crockett served in Congress, a group of members walking up Pennsylvania Avenue was crowded off the street by mountaineers driving a herd of hogs. A congressman from Massachusetts yelled, "There go your constituents, Crockett. Where do you think they're going?"

David quickly shot back, "To Massachusetts, to teach school."

Speaking of hogs, an old mountain story goes something like this: A man went by his neighbor's place and saw him holding a young pig in his arms, raising him up every now and then to eat a fresh apple on the tree. Apples had fallen and were all over the ground, so he said to his neighbor, "Why don't you just let that pig eat those apples on the ground?"

"He likes these better right off the tree," the neighbor replied.

"Well, doesn't that take up a lot of time?" the man insisted.

"What's time to a pig?" was the reply.

Another hog story is about two men arguing over how best to raise hogs. One told the other, "I know hogs; I grew up with hogs." The other replied, "Yeah, and you never got above your raising."

Then there's the one about two good old boys who stole a hog and put it in the seat in the pickup between them. The local police stopped them, and immediately one threw a coat over most of the pig as it sat up in the seat beside them. The lawman asked them their names and where they were from. They told him, "We're the Jackson boys from Gnaw Bone: Jim and Joe." About that time, the hog grunted. The lawman let them go, but later he told his partner, "That Oink Jackson boy shore was ugly, wasn't he?"

A few decades after David Crockett died, Zeb Vance appeared on the North Carolina political scene. He was another colorful, fiddle-playing mountaineer who served his state as both governor and U.S. senator. His wit and humor were just as rambunctious and often as bawdy as that of Crockett. He once made a speech in Washington where he gave a recipe for persimmon brandy and beer, recommending it as an aid to oratory since it would cause one to say less than usual because it "would pucker your mouth."

Once, Vance was following a lady wearing a skirt up a ladder to board a ship. She glanced down at him looking up at her and said, "Sir, you are no gentleman."

Vance quickly replied, "I beg your pardon, Madam, but I can see that you are not either."

Some years later, another North Carolina mountaineer, U.S. Senator Sam Ervin, continued the mountain raconteur tradition when he described some of the over-educated, pompous bureaucrats in the capital city as "people who learn more and more about less and less until they finally come to know everything about nothing." Zeb and David would have got a chuckle out of that.

The first mountain frontiersman to become U.S. president was Andrew Jackson, a tough man known as "Old Hickory" who carried two bullets in his body from early duels. He stood six foot one and weighed 140 pounds. Once when he went to a doctor for bleeding in the lungs, he told him first thing, "I can bear as much as most men, but there are two things I can't give up: one is coffee and the other is tobacco."

During the famous Battle of New Orleans, which helped make Jackson president, the unschooled old warrior from the hills gave the order, "Elevate them guns and shoot a little lower!"

James K. Polk was Jackson's protégé from Tennessee who became president in 1844. A workaholic, he held boring parties in the White House. Senator Sam Houston, a fellow Tennessean and sometimes carouser, said, "The thing that's the matter with Polk is he drinks too much water."

The third mountaineer to become president was Andrew Johnson, also of Tennessee, whom Abraham Lincoln chose as his vice-presidential running mate in 1864. As a senator, Johnson remained loyal to the Union and made speeches opposing secession in Kingsport, Knoxville, and other mountain cities with a revolver laying on the platform within his reach. He said, "I will cling to the Union as a ship-wrecked mariner clings to the last plank while the tempest closes around him."

As transportation gradually improved in the mountains over the years, traveling strangers often came by. They were called "folks-of-the-road" or "hirelings." As the natives would say, "He ain't one of us" or "he don't belong hyar." Later, they might be termed "furriners" or "touristers." If they stayed, they were "move-ins," "transplants," or, in more recent years, "half-backs," referring to Yankees who had gone to Florida and then moved halfway back. Whatever the terminology, in the history of mountain humor, many good yarns point to the ignorance of some outsider or city slicker asking a foolish question:

In Cleveland, Georgia, there used to be two road signs at an intersection. Each pointed in opposite directions and said, "Young Harris, 38 miles." One went over Neels Gap; the other went over Unicoi Gap, but the mileage distance was the same. Somewhat puzzled, a "tourister" pulled his car into a filling station at the fork in the road and approached an old mountaineer in a tilted, straight-back chair. "Does it matter which road I take to Young Harris?" he inquired.

The old man spat out some of his tobacco juice and answered, "Not to me it don't."

Another "tourister" got lost going to Asheville and saw a mountain farmer standing in a pasture. He pulled his car to the side, got out, walked a few feet, and asked, "How far is it to Asheville?"

"Don't know," the farmer bluntly replied and started walking away from the fence.

"You don't know much, do you?" the man in the suit blurted out.

The farmer turned on his heel and answered, "Well, I ain't lost."

This angered the already agitated traveler, who then replied, "There ain't much between you and a fool, is there?"

"No," said the farmer, "just a fence."

The answer to "How far?": "About a hundred times the length of a fool. So why don't you lie down and start measuring?"

"How do you get to Knoxville?" the tourister asked a man in Robbinsville.

"Well, sometimes my boy takes me in his pickup, and sometimes I catch the bus."

Then there's the one about the politician out on the road trying to get a few votes. He saw a young lady in the hallway of a barn milking a cow. He stopped and went over to her. He was asking for her vote when a loud female voice came from the nearby house, "Mary Frances, who is that out there you're talking to?"

"Just a politician, Maw," the young lady answered.

The old lady in the house quickly replied, "Well get yourself in here this minute . . . and bring that cow with you!"

Nearly all mountain families owned a dog or two. It was said that no one was too poor to own a dog, and some families were so poor they owned ten or twelve. Bragging about one's dog was a common pastime.

One day Tom was bragging about how his dog Tojo was so smart that he wouldn't bark when he was chasing a coon across posted land and would also mind Tom. As if to prove his point, Tom called to Tojo laying in the shade a few yards away. "Come here, Tojo," he said. The dog got up, turned, and went under the porch. "Or get under that porch," Tom quickly added.

Another old dog story has a mountaineer telling his friend, "I got a dog for my wife." The friend answered, "I wish I could get a trade like that!"

Many Friday nights, foxhunters got together to take the hounds out to make a little "music" as they chased the elusive animals. It also gave them a chance to drink a little liquor and tell a few lies.

One cool winter night, the hunters built up a bonfire, got pretty deep in the "corn," and all dozed off to sleep. One of the regulars was Old Andy, who had lost the lower part of his leg in a timber accident when a tree fell on him and wore an old wooden peg leg in its place. As he slept, Andy let his wooden leg get in the fire and part of it burned off without him even knowing it.

Suddenly, the dogs struck a trail. Andy jumped up and then fell down the slope of the mountain. The others heard him thrashing around and yelled, "Andy, are you all right?"

"Yeah," came back the drunken answer from Andy, "but watch it; there's a helluva hole every other step down here!"

Wooden legs were fairly common in the old days. Another wooden leg story goes like this: The mountaineer says, "My old wooden leg pained me purdy fierce last night."

His friend responds, "How can a wooden leg hurt?"

The old mountain man answers, "My ole lady hit me over the head with it."

Another hunting story has a native mountaineer taking a new "move-in" deer hunting. They go far back in the mountains to camp out and be at their "stands" early the next morning. Way back "in the middle of nowhere" is a shack where the old man lives who owns the hunting property. The native knows him well but thinks it would be courteous to stop and thank him for letting them hunt on his land. After he does this and is about to leave, the old man asks if the hunter will do him a favor. His old mule is dying and needs to be "put down," but he can't bear to shoot the old animal. Would his friend, he asks, please shoot his old mule for him and spare him that sad duty?

Of course, the hunter says he will, but he decides to play a trick on his innocent new "move-in" friend. When he gets in the truck, he pretends to be mad and says, "That old S.O.B. says we can't hunt on his property. That makes me so mad I think I'll just kill his mule!"

They drive a few yards down the road to the pasture where the mule and two cows are grazing. The man gets out and goes down into the pasture and shoots the mule. Almost as soon as he does, he hears another shot nearby.

"I'm mad, too," his friend says, "so I just shot his cow."

There's another story about a man trading a mule to one of the new "move-ins" in the settlement.

The next day the new owner of the mule returned to tell the man, "That mule you traded me must be blind. I turned it loose in the pasture, and it started running around and ran into a tree. Then it got up and ran into another tree."

"No, it ain't blind," the farmer answered. "It just don't give a damn."

Perhaps the classic "furriner" tale goes like this: A city slicker was driving around on the back roads and went up into the head of a cove where he had to turn around in the yard of an old mountain home. An old man was sitting on the porch chewing tobacco, and every once in a while he would lean way over the front porch to spit. The visitor decided he should perhaps speak to the man and be neighborly. He got out of his car and walked up to the steps, saying, "This is mighty pretty country." The old man nodded, so the visitor continued, "Look at those fields green with corn. And those blue mountains in the distance, they seem to reach to the sky. They're beautiful."

"Yep, it's purdy all right," said the native, "and it's home."

Thinking he had met a friendly man, the "tourister" pushed it a little further. "But they say there's some mighty ignorant people around here."

The old man leaned forward and almost confidentially said, "Don't you fret yourself about that: the first good frost, all them 'furriners' go home!"

There are many stories about old mountain men. One is about the old man who brags, "I ain't got an enemy in the world." When the listener says something like "how wonderful," the old man replies, "Yep, outlived every damn one of them."

Or there's the old mule trader who traded and trafficked in mules, never keeping any mule for long, except for one that he seemed partial to.

It had beautiful long ears and was his favorite. Over time, however, those velvet-like ears grew tattered and torn from rubbing against the rough rafters of its stall in the barn. One day, a neighbor saw the old trader working at the barn, jacking up each side, putting rocks under it, raising the old structure about six inches higher. "Why are you doing that?" the onlooker asks.

"So his ears won't drag on the rafters," the mule trader answered.

Always anxious to tell someone how to do something, the neighbor then asked, "Why don't you just dig out the dirt floor some? That would be the simpler thing to do."

The mule trader, tired of the interruption, looked up with exasperation and answered, "You don't understand nothin'! It ain't the mule's legs that are too long, it's his ears!"

The "advice-giving" nature of some "know-it-alls" is evident in the story of a man who put his boys to work building a rock wall next to the town's post office. "But we don't know nothin' about building walls," the boys complained.

"Don't worry about that," the man replied. "There'll be a dozen folk by here who will tell you how to do it."

Then there's the classic story of one not wanting to admit a mistake. Seems as if a fellow is at the blacksmith shop standing around watching and happens to pick up a red-hot horseshoe, which he quickly drops. The blacksmith looks up and says, "Hot, ain't it?"

The man with the burnt hand answers, "No, it just don't take me long to look at a horseshoe."

Old Zeb told his neighbor, "My boy Bob broke his arm eating supper the other night."

The neighbor quickly asked, "How'd that happen?"

"He fell out of the persimmon tree," came the answer.

There are also many education stories. Here are a few:

The couple scrimped and saved and sent their son off to college. He majored in math, and when he came back home with his degree, his paw couldn't wait to show him off. As quick as he could, he took him down to the country store where his friends often gathered. As they all looked on, the father said, "This boy majored in algebra and has got a degree in it. Say something in algebra to these folks."

The boy, trying to please his folks who had sacrificed so much for his education, said, "Pi-r-squared."

His father stomped one foot and said, "Boy, everybody knows that ain't right. Pie are round. Cornbread are square."

A strapping young boy took a literature class. When the class read Shakespeare's *Macbeth*, the professor bore down heavy on the pre-battle scene where the words go something like this: "Lay on Macduff and damn be he who first cries hold enough."

Later, the mountain boy from Slabtown told his parents about it. He explained, "And they got into this big fight, and one said to the other, 'Lay on Macduff . . . .'" Then the mountain lad paused and started over, "Lay on Macduff, damn if I ain't had enough."

The most outlandish of all these college stories involves the mountain lad who desperately needed some money but knew he had already gone way over his limit and needed to give his dad a big incentive to send a little bit more. So, the story goes, he dreamt up a tall tale.

He wrote his dad that there was a professor who could teach dogs to talk, and wouldn't it be good for Old Ned, his dad's favorite hound, to be able to talk? "The 'fessor could do it for one hundred dollars."

As he thought it would, this got his dad's attention, and here came a letter with the money notifying him Old Ned would be coming by train.

The son looked after the dog and enjoyed spending the money. Then came the end of the school year, and he had to take the beloved old dog home to his waiting Dad.

The boy was in a panic as he headed back home to face his father. Then he thought of an idea, and when he got off the train in Bryson City, he was ready. Quickly, his old dad came running up, hugged him, and, looking around, asked where Old Ned was. The son told this story: "We were coming out of Asheville, and he was sitting by me and started telling me, 'I'll be glad to see your dad, but I hope he's still not carrying on with that woman down the road from the house. I saw them doing some things they ought not to be doing.' And, Dad, that made me so mad I choked that low-down dog to death right then and there and threw him out the window and down the side of the mountain and killed him."

His father, who had first gone pale and then got red-faced, said, "Son, you did the right thing. But, are you shore—I mean *really* shore—that lying dog is dead?"

There are also hundreds of judge stories, for "court week" in any mountain village was often the best entertainment of the year.

There's the judge who asked the mountain witness, "Did you see the altercation?"

"No, Sir," Slim answered, "but I saw one helluva fight!"

Another witness was asked about the veracity of the one on trial, "Have you ever heard his honesty questioned?"

"No, Sir," the witness answered. "I ain't even heard it mentioned."

The witness, an elderly man in overalls, was describing the boundary in a land-line dispute. "It's just a little old creek I can pee halfway across."

The judge lightly pounded his gavel and reprimanded him. "You're out of order, Sir."

The witness didn't hesitate. "I know I'm out of order, Judge. When I was younger and in order, I could pee all the way across it."

Another "judge" story goes like this: A man was charged with making bootleg whiskey. His name was Moses. When he went before the judge, His Honor, trying to poke a little fun, asked, "Are you the Moses who made the waters part?"

"No, Your Honor, I'm the Moses who made the moon shine."

Sometimes the "'shine" was so strong, it would take a pretty tough effort to get it down. The story is told of one man being asked to point a gun at his friend to "force" him to take a drink. Then, after his gulp, the other man said, "Now, hold that gun on me."

Here are three stories about old mountain doctors:

Jake, getting up in years, goes to see the old mountain doctor, complaining, "I'm getting so hard of hearing, I can't hear myself poot."

The doc pulls out a drawer and gives the old fellow a handful of large pills.

"Will these help me hear better?" Jake asks.

"I don't know," the doc replies, "but they'll make you poot louder."

Another old-timer complained of losing his hearing, and the doctor reminded him that "all that whiskey you drink is what's the problem."

The man thought of the alternative and replied, "Well, Doc, I like what I've been drinking so much more than what I've been hearing, I guess I'll just go on getting deef."

Another time, the doc gave Ole Tom some pills with the instructions to take one pill with a small drink of whiskey every day.

A few weeks later, they met at the store, and the doc asked Tom how he was feeling. Tom replied, "Purdy good, considering I'm a week behind on the pills and three weeks ahead on the whiskey."

A frequently told story about hardship in the mountains is the classic one about a little widow-woman who lived alone, far back on an almost impassable dirt road at the "end of nowhere." One winter a particularly deep snow covered the entire area, and all travel—by foot, jeep, or horseback—was extremely difficult. After about a week of these conditions, a four-wheeler finally got a Red Cross worker to her isolated cabin. The worker went to her door, fearing the worst. He began, "I'm from the Red Cross . . ." and before he could go any further, the little woman replied, "I'm afraid I can't help you this time. We've had a pretty rough winter." Such was the spirit of these hardy souls.

Sometime before World War II, a mountain congressman from Arkansas was invited to a big social function at the Mayflower Hotel in Washington. He happened to be seated next to Emily Post, the famous expert on etiquette and social behavior. As the dinner began, he extended his hand and said to the social queen, "My name is Brooks Hayes, congressman from Arkansas. What's your'n?"

She looked down her nose and said, "I'm Emily Post."

"Glad to know you, Miz Post," he replied and then added, "'Cuse me, Ma'am, but you're eating my salad."

When the Tennessee Valley Authority brought electricity to many in the mountains, it changed their way of life. There's an old story about the board of deacons at a local Baptist church discussing buying a chandelier for the sanctuary. The oldest deacon there, who was in his eighties and could barely hear the discussion, did hear the motion "to buy a chandelier." The frugal old man exclaimed, "Hold on a minute. Where are we going to order it from, who can even spell it, and if we get it, who can play it? If you ask me, we need a light fixture a lot more!"

A similar story has a traveling salesman coming by and telling the man of the house, "Now that you've got kids in school, you need to buy them an encyclopedia."

"No, Siree," the man answered. "Let 'em walk to school like I did!"

These jokes are only a sampling of mountain humor, or "poking fun" as it is often called. Poking fun at the pompous, the pretentious, and often at oneself tells a lot about the people of the hills who have always valued a good chuckle. That's why this chapter was included. For, as the Pulitzer Award-winning poet and novelist Stephen Vincent Benét wrote, "It always seemed to me that legends and yarns and tales are as much a part of the real history of a country as proclamations and provisos and constitutions."

And so it seems to me.

CHAPTER 11

Whose Mountains?

That is the question. Just whose mountains are they anyway? God made them and took His time in perfecting them. For tens of millions of years they were the sole domain of His marvelous creatures, many now extinct. Man, in his early forms, then claimed them as his own. More recently came the Native Americans, and until about 300 years ago, they mostly had this paradise to themselves.

The white man—tough, independent, resilient, and born to fight—came next, and when these men met the mountains, it was a marriage made in heaven.

One hundred years ago, timber barons discovered the seemingly unending lush forests. Armed with their saws and axes and encouraged by settlers anxious to make money and stay close to home, combined with the outside world's hunger for building materials, they scalped much of the mountains' exteriors. Then the coal companies ate away at their insides, both groups leaving the region cut and bleeding.

Then came the hydroelectric engineers with their promise of progress. Armed with the skill to do something unthought of only a few years before, they tamed the mighty rivers of the region and brought the marvel of electricity to millions who had lived in darkness more than a third of their twenty-four-hour days, save for the flickering flame of a fireplace, or later a kerosene lamp.

Then, in 1960 an unlikely visitor came to the region. His intent, like those who came before him, was to take something from the area. Not timber, not buckskins, not coal or timber, not their homes and farms that remained to be covered with water—no, all this interloper wanted was their vote. He got it, and in so doing showed the nation the tolerance and hospitality of a forgotten people found in this heretofore largely ignored region.

Next came a Texan with big ideas and so many programs that it was impossible to keep up with them. Just like Lyndon Johnson had once picked up his beagles by their ears, so he lifted the area with money, roads, and programs. He was generous without question, but frequently the carrots came with sticks, and often those in charge had only one way to do things: their way. Still, Santa LBJ filled many stockings and left many goodies, some of which have lasted to this day.

During this time, and still to some extent today, no subject could raise the ire of the mountaineer more quickly than that of the programs of the "giverment," which he perceived as an attempt to deny him full and free exercise of what he regarded were his God-given rights of person and property.

His experience with the federal programs created to protect, preserve, and transform his cherished mountains have given him cause in his own mind to be wary of the "furriners." When Uncle Sam came in proposing to improve his life and habitat, it would always raise the mountianeer's unbridled, independent spirit. The native viewed these outsiders in terms of how they impacted his personal life, home, and property. Many were not concerned with how this activity could save the region's scenic and natural resources from exploitation and destruction.

Today, our imagination is staggered by the realization of what clearly would have been the fate of our southern mountains and their magnificent trees, incomparable ridges and valleys, and admirable people had the federal government not intervened early in the twentieth century.

Many of the outside interests, in pursuit of the quick buck, plundered the timber and mineral resources of the region at the beginning of the twentieth century and the decades afterward. Left to their own greedy machinations, they would have turned this treasure of natural wealth and beauty into a vast wasteland of charred tree stumps, eroded and scarred mountainsides, and polluted streams from which it might have never recovered.

During the logging boom that began in the 1880s and continued into the 1920s, trees were harvested without any regard for other resources or future timber supplies. Young growth was damaged or destroyed, and smaller limbs and brush were left to ignite into wildfires during dry spells.

In many locations, entire mountainsides were cut and burned, and hillsides were left vulnerable to the ravages of erosion. In these places, the soil became leached, and the streams dried up in the fall and became raging floods in the spring. Most accessible forests were depleted.

Mountain families, unaccustomed to dealing in cash and unfamiliar with timber and mineral rights and deeds, sold their land for astonishingly low prices or lost it to unscrupulous agents who found they had inexact or missing titles or bought them up for unpaid back taxes.

All of that was minor in comparison to the destruction that mining, particularly for coal, inflicted upon the mountain environment. Mountainsides were ripped open by strip-mining and often abandoned when depleted. The demand for wooden pit props, poles, and railroad ties resulted in extinction of the surrounding forests, and the mines produced slag heaps and acid mine runoff that severely damaged streams and wildlife.

Even worse was the human exploitation of cheap mountain labor and the herding of displaced mountain farm families into isolated "company towns." There, they suffered serious health hazards and intolerable living conditions and lived in virtual bondage to the company-owned stores.

Not only was the independent family-farming existence that had characterized the southern mountains seriously disrupted, but also the environment of the highlands was severely damaged. In many places, the entire economy and society of the mountains was significantly altered, and virtually all the profits of this exploitation were taken outside the region. With few exceptions, the capitalists who invested in Appalachian enterprises back then did so only to extract the desired riches and then withdraw.

Ironically, one of the tycoons of the Post-Civil War era, who might have been expected to profiteer from the situation, provided the example and initial financing for helping to resolve the problem. Through the establishment and maintenance of a system of renewable national forests administered by the "hated" federal government, George W. Vanderbilt in 1889 began purchasing, assembling, and developing the vast 100,000-acre North Carolina Estate near Asheville that was to become the renowned site of the palatial Biltmore House. The nation's first School of Forestry and the tract of cutover woodlands were restored into the showcase forest, which eventually became the nucleus of what is now the acclaimed Pisgah National Forest.

It was also Vanderbilt who first hired and encouraged Gilbert Pinchot, who was to become the first head of the U.S. Forest Service and later regarded as the father of scientific forestry. Vanderbilt also brought to America the German forester Carl Alwin Schenck, who developed the techniques of reforestation of culled and eroded areas of the south with eastern, white, pitch, and short-leaf pines that prevail to this date.

Congress, in 1891, inspired by preservationists like Henry Thoreau and Sierra Club founder John Muir and Utilitarians like Vanderbilt, Pinchot, and Schenck, amended the General Land Law Revision Act to give the U.S. president almost unlimited power to withdraw huge expanses of forested lands from the public domain as national reserves.

In 1900, the Division of Forestry and the Geological Survey conducted a field investigation of the situation in the Southern Appalachian Region and submitted a report that decried the widespread damage of destructive lumbering. They recommended the establishment of a federal forest reserve in Southern Appalachia as the only way to stop the alarming loss of the nation's future timber resources there. That report merely gathered dust until President Theodore Roosevelt sent it to Congress for action some years later in the wake of a series of disastrous floods on the Monongahela and Ohio rivers in 1907.

Pioneering legislation authorizing the secretary of agriculture to purchase land for forest reserves in the eastern United States where there was no public domain was sponsored by Massachusetts Congressman John Weeks and signed by President William Howard Taft on March 1, 1911. The law invoked a broad and unique interpretation of the Interstate Commerce Clause of the U.S. Constitution to permit the acquisition of "such forested, cutover, or denuded lands within the watersheds of navigable streams as . . . may be necessary to the regulation of the flow of navigable streams."

While it did not so specify, the legislation implied that those purchases were to be made in the Southern Appalachians and the White Mountains of New England and made an initial appropriation of $11 million for that purpose. The National Forest Reservation Commission, composed of members of the Cabinet and Congress, hit the ground running and within the month authorized the establishment of thirteen purchase units, seven of which were in our southern mountains and were increased to eleven the following year.

The goal of assembling reserves of 5,000,000 acres in Southern Appalachia and 600,000 acres in the White Mountains was adopted. The first purchase approved was a 31,000-acre tract in Fannin, Union, Lumpkin, and Gilmer counties of Georgia at $7 per acre. The first tract actually purchased was an 8,100-acre tract in McDowell County, North Carolina, for $7.25 an acre.

President Woodrow Wilson proclaimed the first national forest assembled under the Weeks Act in October 1916. Appropriately, it was the Pisgah National Forest, encompassing the developed holdings of George Vanderbilt, which were sold to the federal government by his widow for $433,500.

In 1918, the Natural Bridge National Forest was created in western Virginia, and four more were proclaimed in 1930—the Boone in North Carolina, the Nantahala in North and South Carolina and Georgia, the Cherokee in Tennessee, and the Unaka in Tennessee, North Carolina, and Virginia. Later, the Boone was joined to the Pisgah in 1921 and the Unaka partitioned among the Pisgah, Jefferson, and Cherokee in 1923 and 1936.

Until 1936, when the Chattahoochee National Forest was established in Georgia, the boundaries of these forests were fluid and constantly changing. This resulted from new legislation authorizing the agriculture secretary to obtain land for swaps of titles or timber and to make purchases outside of navigable river headwaters.

By the end of the 1930 fiscal year, 4,133,484 of the targeted 5,000,000 acres in the south had been acquired. The National Forest Reservation Commission decided not to exercise its power of eminent domain, and all the acquisitions were obtained through purchase or negotiated transaction, principally from logging and lumber companies eager to rid themselves of tracts that either were already cutover or found inaccessible.

Individual landowners, having learned from their bitter experiences with the profiteers, became more sophisticated negotiators and traders and generally fared well in their dealings with the Forest Service. Some chose to accept lower prices in return for lifetime tenure agreements permitting them to stay on their land until their deaths.

The effects of the first purchases were declines in population growth and in both the number and acreage of farms, the latter dropping 39 and 22 percent respectively in Rabun and Fannin counties in Georgia, for example. Two problems came to the fore immediately: the loss of the property tax base by the counties in which the acquired forest acreage was located and the resistance of the mountain people to federal regulations and programs to prevent and control forest fires.

The commission addressed the first by providing that 5 percent (later 25 percent) of all receipts from sales on national forest lands within a county would go to that county for schools and roads. But the issue did not go away even though Congress finally sought to resolve it with the passage of the Payments in Lieu of Taxes Act in 1976, which established a formula guaranteeing counties with national forest lands at least 75 cents per acre per year in compensation of tax losses on them.

As for fires, it was a characteristic of mountain people, learned from the Indians, to "green up" their lands and hold down the populations of "snakes and varmints" by burning the woods. Often this resulted in devastating forest fires, which put the mountaineers into immediate conflict with the Forest Service that was responsible for preventing such fires.

The mountain man has always had a hard time understanding why he could not do what he pleased with his own land. While great progress has been made through education and the employment of native mountaineers as forest rangers, the Forest Service continues to battle the problem of woods burning. Until recent decades, the Forest Service had continuing encounters also with mountain moonshiners who persisted in locating their stills in the remote coves of the national forests.

About the time Vanderbilt, Pinchot, and Schenck were succeeding with their forestry experiments at Biltmore, Dr. Chase P. Ambler of Asheville organized the Appalachian National Park Association. Its goal was to create an eastern equivalent of the first national park established at Yellowstone in 1872 within the Great Smoky Mountains of North Carolina and Tennessee. Pushing this project continued for more than three decades.

Two issues slowed the process. First, the plans competed with the efforts of the Forest Service to establish a national forest within that region. Principally, though, they were thwarted because of the opposition of the timber interests, which controlled 85 percent of the area, and the inaccessibility of most of the region.

Progress finally took place at a dinner held at the prestigious Cosmos Club in Washington, D.C., by Congressman Zebulon Weaver of Asheville in December 1923. This meeting resulted in the appointment of a Southern Appalachian National Park Study Committee by the U.S. secretary of the interior early the following year. Shortly afterward came the organization of the Great Smoky Mountains Conservation Association in Knoxville, Tennessee, and the establishment of park commissions by the states of North Carolina and Tennessee.

The campaign for public support and contributions was highly successful, fueled by the articles and speeches of Horace Kephart, the acknowledged Boswell of the Southern Highlands. Also helpful were the editorial campaigns of publishers Charles A. Webb of the *Asheville Citizen and Times* and Edward Meeman of the *Knoxville News-Sentinel.* It bore fruit in the passage of a bill authorizing federal parks to be established in the Blue Ridge and Great Smoky Mountains, which was signed in 1926 by President Calvin Coolidge.

The measure provided that the Great Smoky Mountains National Park was to be comprised of 704,000 acres purchased by state and private funds. The new National Park Service, created a decade earlier, would assume its administration once 150,000 acres were purchased and its operation as soon as a minimum of 300,000 acres were turned over to the federal government.

North Carolina and Tennessee appropriated $2 million and $1.5 million respectively for the purchase, and John D. Rockefeller, Jr., gave $5 million to match contributions on a dollar-for-dollar basis. The first tract was purchased jointly by the city of Knoxville and the state of Tennessee, a 76,507-acre parcel for which the Little River Lumber Company was paid $3.57 per acre.

The lumber companies bitterly fought the effort to make it a national park. The Smokies, at that time, constituted the largest area of original forest remaining in the eastern United States. One-third of its surface was still primeval forest, so this region with its unequalled tree cover was a logger's paradise.

The state commissions were forced to resort to costly and time-consuming condemnation suits, the last of which was not resolved until the 1940s. The most notorious suit was against the Champion Fiber Company of North Carolina, and it eventually had to be resolved by the arbitration of the National Park Service director who finally got the parties to settle on a figure of $32 per acre for a total of $3 million for the 92,824.5-acre tract.

While most individual landowners were willing, if not eager, to sell their holdings, perhaps the most famous condemnation case of all was that involving Cades Cove, Tennessee, a wide valley of farms passed down for several generations from the original settlers, surrounded by some of the Smokies' highest peaks and containing its most varied virgin deciduous forest, with some trees more than 300 years old.

Farmer John Oliver successfully fought condemnation from 1929 until 1935 and eventually was paid $45 per acre for his 375 acres. Many of his neighbors were relieved from such adamant opposition by agreements allowing them to be lifetime tenants of their property and an understanding that the community would be preserved as a historical area and serve as a major showpiece of the park.

The timber interests sought to confuse, divide, and sidetrack the proponents by reviving the national forest idea as an alternative to a park. But the idea for a Great Smoky Mountains National Park proved to be one for which the time had come. Its headquarters opened in Gatlinburg, Tennessee, in 1931.

The National Park Service assumed responsibility for its administration and future land acquisition when 400,000 acres were deeded to it in 1936, and President Franklin D. Roosevelt dedicated the park itself in 1940. During World War II, it received a great boost in size when the Tennessee Valley Authority transferred to the park some 44,000 acres it had acquired for the building of Fontana Dam.

Although the economic boom predicted by park enthusiasts was slow to arrive, the park developed into one of the most popular in the nation. Gatlinburg and Pigeon Forge, with Dollywood Amusement Park, have virtually exploded into a major resort for both summer and winter tourists.

Less controversial was the establishment of the Shenandoah National Park and the building of its spectacular Skyline Drive in Virginia. This made inevitable the proposal for a parkway that would connect them with the Great Smoky Mountains National Park to the south. In 1930, Kentucky Congressman Maurice Thatcher first advanced this idea, and it was then pushed forward at a meeting at the Virginia governor's mansion in September 1933, when Virginia senator Harry F. Byrd convinced U.S. Secretary of the Interior Harold Ickes of its worth and feasibility.

Later, President Roosevelt enthusiastically embraced the idea as a major project to be funded by a $4 million appropriation after the purchasing of the necessary 200-foot right-of-way by the states of North Carolina and Virginia. Secretary Ickes assigned the parkway to the jurisdiction of the National Park Service, which was to utilize the services of the Civilian Conservation Corps.

Condemnation proceedings for the 38,000 acres of right-of-way in North Carolina and 23,500 acres in Virginia were as heatedly contested and time-consuming as those for Cades Cove lands in the Smokies. Actual construction began in September 1935 with the employment of 100 men from the relief rolls of Alleghany County, North Carolina. It was not completed until after World War II.

Secretary Ickes also had to step in and settle the bitter wrangling between the states of North Carolina and Tennessee. He chose a route following the higher mountain ridge in North Carolina by Grandfather Mountain and Asheville and entering the Great Smoky Park at Cherokee, North Carolina. Because the route bypassed the populated areas of the Southern Appalachians and the park service forbade commercial development along it, the people of the Southern Highlands actually benefited little aside from the sale of land and the Depression employment the construction provided.

Although it did little to preserve the culture or immediately enhance the economy, the route did develop into one of the most stupendous drives in the world. Today, people can enjoy the scenic vistas of the Great Blue Ridge and its sister Smokies without having to leave the comfort of their automobiles or having their views obscured by a single commercial billboard.

Even less commercial but highly popular is the famed 2,100-mile Appalachian Trail, the rugged hiking route extending from Georgia's Springer Mountain to Maine's Mount Katahdin. Its development dates also from the advocacy of Horace Kephart in the late 1920s.

Initial development of the trail happened in disjointed and sporadic spurts under the auspices of various federal, state, and private agencies and organizations. Perhaps the most valuable work and significant contributions were made by the Civilian Conservation Corps during the course of its Depression Era existence and by the U.S. Forest Service. If it had not been for the unrelenting efforts of the Appalachian Trail Conference, a group of trail enthusiasts, the Appalachian Trail might never have come to fruition.

Like all the other Depression-fighting programs of the New Deal, the Civilian Conservation Corps (CCC) had its critics, but its major contributions remain to this day. This quasi-military labor force known as "Roosevelt's Tree Army" did outstanding work with lasting benefits in the improvement, protection, and preservation of the forests of our southern mountains.

This is especially true when in its later years the majority of the group's ranks was composed of local youths who felt at home in the mountain environment of the Southland. They engaged in tree planting, timber stand improvement, recreation development, road and trail building, telephone line installation, and scores of related jobs and also attended both academic and vocational educational classes.

The truck trails or "fire roads" and the fire towers they built were major factors in the development of the Forest Service's effective programs for combating forest fires and also many of the recreational facilities of the Great Smoky Mountains and Shenandoah national parks. The Blue Ridge Parkway and the public access areas bordering the lakes of the Tennessee Valley Authority (TVA) were their handiwork. Many of them grew so skilled that they subsequently qualified for permanent employment with the Forest Service. A measure of the overall popularity and acceptance of the CCC was the fact that when the emergency legislation establishing it expired in March 1937, Congress passed new legislation to continue it.

The onset of World War II necessitated its disbandment, but memories of the CCC's contributions and benefits still prompt calls for its reactivation when, from time to time, unemployment numbers increase or the question of universal military service arises. The great advantage the CCC enjoyed over other New Deal "make-work" programs is that it did "real" work with obvious benefits.

More controversial was the Tennessee Valley Authority and the dislocation it caused by flooding the valleys of the Tennessee River and its tributaries with waters impounded by mammoth hydroelectric dams in the states of Tennessee, Kentucky, North Carolina, Georgia, and Alabama. Since all of its acquisitions of land were by condemnation and the implementation of its projects required the total evacuation of the areas to be flooded, mountain people at first resisted the TVA, as they were displaced from homes many of their families had occupied for generations. Of course, in the long run the region benefited greatly from the availability of cheap electricity and the resulting industrial, economic, and recreational development.

Perhaps no TVA project generated more economic impact than the building of the Fontana Dam on the Little Tennessee River high in the mountains of Swain and Graham counties, North Carolina. The dam was rushed to completion on a round-the-clock construction schedule during World War II to generate power for war industries. It featured construction of a model town of 6,000 known as Fontana Village and impounded a mammoth lake that is a popular recreation destination today.

The dam was not completed, however, until November 1944, only a few months before the end of the war, so its initial purpose was largely unrealized. The controversies created when its floodwaters inundated roads that were not replaced and separated churches and cemeteries from the communities they served continued for many years. As previously mentioned, the TVA also deeded large tracts of the original land it had bought to the Great Smoky Mountains National Park.

The dislocation created by the establishment of the uranium-processing facilities for the atomic bomb at Oak Ridge, Tennessee, is probably without parallel insofar as the concentrated impact upon the population and property of a compact area is concerned. In 1941, the Army Corps of Engineers swooped into the 59,000-acre Oak Ridge region west of Knoxville, condemned all of the land, and forced the immediate evacuation of nearly a thousand bewildered and resentful mountain families. They were given orders to move in October, and between then and November, they met a flood of incoming construction workers and equipment as they left. To add insult to injury, the natives did not know for more than four years the reason they were forced to relocate permanently from their ancestral homes and their cherished community.

World War II brought a temporarily booming economy to our southern mountains as the natural resources of the region—timber, coal, and water power—were in high demand and a labor supply to marshal them was short. Prices and wages were generally high for men and women who were able to get and hold the available jobs.

In many areas, these events signaled the beginning of the end of an agricultural economy and set the stage for the depression that settled over most of the area when war mobilization wound down, defense plants closed, and the coal and timber industries all but shut down.

The resultant hardcore poverty shocked President John F. Kennedy when he came into Appalachia to campaign for the presidency in the crucial West Virginia primary of 1960. It also prompted many of the initiatives of his New Frontier and most of the programs of President Lyndon B. Johnson's Great Society and War on Poverty.

These programs were numerous and included an Accelerated Public Works Program, the Area Development Administration, the Manpower Development and Training Act, the Appalachian Road Program, and the rejuvenated land acquisition program of the U.S. Forest Service. There was also the multitude of agencies created under the Economic Opportunity Act of 1964, beginning with the Office of Economic Opportunity and continuing with the Community Action Programs, Job Corps, Neighborhood Youth Corps, Volunteers in Service to America (VISTA), Head Start and Summer Head Start, Work Experience and Training Program, and others.

Of most significance to Southern Appalachia was the passage of the Appalachian Regional Development Act of 1965 and the creation of the Appalachian Regional Commission composed of the governors of twelve southeastern and northeastern states. The commission was charged with coordinating the administration of a great new federal-state funding effort for Appalachian development, with emphasis upon the establishment and construction of a system of developmental highways for the region. It also encouraged timber development through both expanded national forests and private enterprise, including expansion and development of outdoor recreational opportunities.

Between 1966 and 1977, ARC spent more than $3.5 billion on such programs, most of which went into highways that opened the region both to tourists and new residents. However, the U.S. General Accounting Office criticized it for "failing to reach the region's critically poor" and "bypassing the hard-core, neediest Appalachian communities." The two counties receiving the most ARC funds between 1966 and 1980 were Wise County, Virginia, with $13 million and Whitfield County, Georgia, with $10 million. All others received less than $8 million.

National forests were expanded considerably during this period. Major acquisitions were made for the Monongahela National Forest in

West Virginia and Kentucky, and the Cumberland National Forest in Kentucky was renamed the Daniel Boone National Forest and greatly enlarged. A law in 1960 required for the first time that national forests be managed for a variety of purposes and set forth five co-equal uses for the nation's forest reserves: outdoor recreation, range (grazing for domestic livestock), timber, watershed, and wildlife and fish.

The National Forest Management Act of 1976 made a major change in acquisition procedures by abolishing the National Forest Reservation Commission and giving the secretary of agriculture the authority to acquire forestlands, subject to the review and approval of the House and Senate agriculture committees.

Also settled was the controversy that arose when ecologists and preservationists won litigation attacking the practice of harvesting timber in national forests by "clear-cutting" or, in the terminology of foresters, "even-aged management."

The inherent opposition of southern mountaineers to encroachment upon their personal independence and property rights, particularly from the federal government, continued to be enflamed by the enactments of the Outdoor Recreation Act, the Wilderness Act, and the Wild and Scenic Rivers Act.

Even so, today our southern mountains offer almost 7 million acres in national forests, parks, and recreation areas.

Acknowledgments

I am very fortunate. In my hometown, the wonderful Mountain Regional Library offers a mother lode of Appalachian lore that I never tire of mining. Back in the secluded stacks and far reaches of its bowels, I found much content for this book and solace for my soul. I thank all of the kind and helpful staff who work there.

When I was a barefoot boy growing up in the southern mountains before the time of television and without a male companion at home, I spent many hours hanging around what the townsfolk called "the loafer's bench" at the country store. Every night, a dozen or so men would gather there after a day's work in the fields or woods to gossip, talk politics, and tell tall tales. In the summer, it was outside on a bench and on nail kegs; in the winter, inside around a potbellied stove. The faces of the "regulars" changed as they came and went, but their conversations, even when their stories were outrageous lies, always fascinated me.

My mother was horrified by the whole business. She was afraid I'd learn cuss words, and I did—a whole vocabulary of them, some so quaint and provincial that when I used them after leaving the mountains, nobody knew what I was talking about.

But I learned more, much of which is in this book, from those interesting characters and friends of long ago. In the theater of my mind I often replay that "once upon a time," realizing with each passing day that I am more a part of that world than the complicated and computerized world of today.

My great-great-grandfather, Thompson Collins, came into the mountains of North Georgia from Buncombe County, North Carolina, in the 1820s. He moved his family into the newly formed Union County in 1832 as the Cherokees were being moved out. He located in the valley of "Choestoe," Cherokee for "land of the dancing rabbits."

Two cousins share my age and the same ancestry and geography. These men, Eric England and Franklin Hunter, still live in that beautiful valley located between Brasstown Bald and Blood Mountain. Both are career military: Eric, a Marine, and Franklin, Air Force, and both came back home after their service.

We three and another mountain friend, Tom Arline, get together every other Friday for what my wife calls "lunch for a few good men," since three of us are Marines. Mostly we talk about our kinfolks, the way they lived and the stories they handed down to us. Much of that is also in this book, and I am grateful for the precious memories we share.

Then there is Hoyle Bryson, my uncle and next-door neighbor, who has lived his ninety-five years in this valley, except for a couple of summers he spent playing professional baseball. He is a direct descendant of the first white man to come into our valley and stay. There's not a trail or ridge or hollow Hoyle has not hunted and trapped, and I've picked his marvelous memory for hundreds of hours. That is also part of this book.

When I write a book, someone always has the difficult chore of deciphering my handwritten words. This time that job fell to the highly competent Misty Aquarian, who did it perfectly and patiently while offering much helpful advice.

My sister, Jane Ross, who lives next door and is a former teacher, read the copy and made many helpful suggestions, as did my son, Matt Miller, and his wife, Katie. My friend, Byron McCombs, is responsible for the photograph on the back cover.

Finally, my wife, Shirley, who has helped me give birth to eight books, was again the "granny woman" for this one. She grew up in the Nantahalas with strong mountain and Cherokee kin who lived the old mountain way. I thank my best critic and most constant cheerleader—again.

I am grateful for all this help, and quickly add that the errors in this work are mine alone.

Zell Miller
Young Harris, Georgia
December 2008

Appendix

101 Reasons Why I Live in Appalachia

1. "I will lift up mine eyes unto the hills, from whence cometh my help." Psalm 121:1

2. "The old home place" is considered hallowed ground.

3. No gnats.

4. "Braveheart" was our ancestor.

5. Dogs ride in the front seat of your pickup.

6. People wish you a "Merry Christmas," not "Happy Holidays."

7. The people never shirk from a challenge of any kind.

8. If your car slides off in a ditch, just wait a few minutes and a good old boy will come by with a logging chain and pull you out.

9. You can understand the words in our songs.

10. Boiled peanuts.

11. Nicknames abound and don't have to be politically correct, such as "Shorty," Nub," "Fuzz." "Bud" is considered a term of endearment.

12. There are four very distinct seasons.

13. When folks ask, "How are you?" they really want to know.

14. Corn production has long been measured by the gallon, not the bushel, as it was even before ethanol came along.

15. Appalachian originals like Patsy Cline, Loretta Lynn, Patty Loveless, and, of course, Mother Maybelle.

16. Drivers always pull over for a funeral procession.

17. Nursing homes are a last resort.

18. The Shenandoah National Park and the Great Smokey Mountain National Park, connected by that scenic old jewel, the Blue Ridge Parkway.

19. "Ain't" ain't laughed at. Neither is "I aim to," meaning intend.

20. Green beans cooked for a long, long time and seasoned with "fat-back" or "streak-of-lean."

21. "Cat-head biscuits" with sourwood honey, sorghum syrup, or apple butter.

22. Autumn in all its glory is a picture no artist can paint.

23. Modesty is a way of life. Or, if there is bragging, it's usually so out-landish that the natives just grin.

24. Our mountains are older than the Rockies, Alps, or Himalayas.

25. It ain't far to the Grand Ole Opry.

26. Old quilts tell a story.

27. The fishing is good in creeks, lakes, rivers, or ponds for trout, bream, crappie, and even catfish.

28. It's okay to use double nouns like biscuit-bread, widow-woman, menfolk, hose-pipe, and "kid-of-a-boy."

29. Adult males do not wear caps turned backwards or sideways.

30. It's where everyone stands when the flag passes or the national anthem is played.

31. Dolly is one of us, and whatever she does or wears we still love her.

32. In these ancient mountains are 2,000 kinds of plants, 150 species of trees, and 200 different kinds of birds.

33. When John Muir, the great naturalist, came through in 1867, he observed that the mountain forests "must have been a great delight for God, for they are the best He ever made."

34. There are many places where cell phones will not work. Thank goodness!

35. Mountaineers have always been among the first to go when a war came along. Citations for bravery have been plentiful among

them, but they'd never tell you about it. Remember Sergeant Alvin York?

36. It is the birthplace of many drivers who built NASCAR.

37. Perhaps the principal feature of the region, the seventy-year-old Appalachian Trail, 2,176 miles from Springer Mountain, Georgia, to Mount Katahdin, Maine.

38. Mist rising from the streams and lakes in the early morning hours.

39. The old tune "Wildwood Flower" played on an autoharp.

40. The toe-tapping music of banjo and fiddle and old-fashioned square-dancing: "Put the birdie in the cage, birdie out, hoot owl in, hoot owl out and gone again."

41. Where mountain sayings like "I'm coming 'dreckly" make perfectly good sense.

42. The sensitive poetry of Byron Herbert Reece: "From chips and shards in idle times / I made these stories, shaped these rhymes. May they engage some friendly tongue / When I am past the reach of song."

43. Where every town has a "loafers' bench" or coffee crowd who solve the problems of the world each morning.

44. Where the first "gold rush" in the nation occurred, twenty years before the 49ers in California. Some say there's still some left. Also rubies.

45. The allure of caves and caverns, more than 2,000 of them, in all shapes and sizes from the Lost Sea near Sweetwater, Tennessee, to a 600-foot-deep pit near Chattanooga.

46. Home remedies for everything from digestive disorders to colds to pimples. Chew sassafras to stop smoking. Calm your nerves with sourwood tea.

47. There's not much hugging among males unless they are family members.

48. Ferns and mossy rocks along streams far back in coves where the sun seldom shines.

49. Jefferson, Jackson, and Lincoln were born here.

50. Where one can know your third cousin, maybe even a double second cousin, and there are old-timers who remember and can tell you about your great-grandpa.

51. Where folks eat squirrel, raccoons, and 'possums, and love dumplings.

52. There's a gun in every home. And in many pickups.

53. Where little streams become mighty raging rivers.

54. Only a few miles from my home I can straddle the headwaters of what becomes the great Chattahoochee River.

55. Monticello, The Hermitage, the Biltmore Estate and the Lincoln cabin birthplace are all part of our architecture.

56. The beauty, thrill, and hidden danger of whitewater. But *not* the kind of danger that the snide James Dickey scared you with in *Deliverance.*

57. Swinging bridges, covered bridges, and foot logs.

58. "Sawmill gravy" made from crumbled-up fried sausage, flour, and milk.

59. "Red-eye gravy" made from the juices of salt-cured country ham mixed with black coffee.

60. Fried pies eaten by hand.

61. Dried fruit stack cake.

62. Mother Nature's air conditioning.

63. The pungent smell of ramps that linger for days.

64. The Appalachian storytelling tradition: funny, sad, insightful, and the clever way it "punctures the pompous."

65. The nip of the first frost.

66. The first robin in the spring.

67. The sad call of the whippoorwill.

68. The incessant chatter of the katydid.

69. The beckoning call of the bobwhite.

70. The profusion of wildflowers.

71. Baptizings, where the saved really go under for the Lord, in old mill ponds or the still waters at a special spot in the river used for generations.

72. Family reunions, all-day singings, and dinner on the grounds.

73. When a male gets a haircut, it's called "getting your ears lowered."

74. Where front porches are still used to "sit a spell."

75. Where feuds are fierce and long in duration. Ask the Hatfields and McCoys. There's a saying: "Insult a Yankee and he'll sue you. Insult a mountaineer and he'll kill you."

76. Where kids still go barefoot.

77. Where recent arrivals are welcome and cordially treated, but will always be known as "move-ins."

78. That great, gutsy mountain spirit. "Mountaineers are always free" is West Virginia's motto.

79. Old cemeteries, weathered tombstones with inscriptions like "She did what she could."

80. The quiet solitude of the forests.

81. For us older mountaineers, there is a greater appreciation for indoor plumbing since we grew up with the inconvenience of an outhouse.

82. Stubborn and stoic people in abundance.

83. The Cherohala Parkway from Robbinsville, North Carolina, to Tellico Plains, Tennessee, with many vistas where the wilderness stretches as far as the eye can see.

84. Being "pushy" is frowned upon.

85. The musical and captivating cadence of a self-taught mountain preacher truly touched by the Lord.

86. My hometown is in a valley surrounded by the Chattahoochee National Forest with its 750,000 acres and ten wilderness areas. All this beauty is protected from the greed of man, as are several million acres in all of Appalachia. The Monongahela National Forest in West Virginia alone includes more than 900,000 acres.

87. Those exalted 400-year-old trees in the lush Joyce Kilmer Memorial Forest.

88. The incomparable Natural Bridge still as grand as in the days when George Washington surveyed it and Thomas Jefferson owned it.

89. Cumberland Falls, the "Niagara of the South," with its 125-foot-wide transparent curtain of water plunging some 65 feet in Whitney County, Kentucky.

90. The Foxfire Center and Museum in Mountain City, Georgia, and all our heritage it celebrates.

91. I live at the foot of Brasstown Bald Mountain, one of some eighty upland ridges from Virginia south that have treeless areas at their summits. Some of these balds are grassy, alpine meadows; others have small scrubby bushes. There is a Rough Butt Bald in North Carolina.

92. The diverse and enduring Georgia Mountain Fair in Hiawassee, Georgia, that has helped explain our mountain heritage for more than a half-century.

93. One place that today's media should visit and study is the Appalachian Cultural Museum in Boone, North Carolina. Its primary purpose is to debunk Appalachian stereotypes. My old friend, the late Cratis William, bless his heart, is largely responsible for it.

94. I can leave my home after breakfast and by lunchtime be in the middle of an authentic Appalachian farm and village of yesteryear. It is the Museum of Appalachia, lovingly and beautifully put together by John Rice Irvin in Norris, Tennessee.

95. "Green-up time" when we go out and gather wild greens such as "polk sallet" and field cress, or "cresses" as it is called. One usually picks a "mess."

96. There are plenty of yard sales.

97. I live less than an hour from places like Hanging Dog, Bugscuffle, Bug Snort, Shake Rag, Granny Squirrel Gap, Chunky Gal

Mountain, Raw Dough, War Woman, Bad Creek, and Worse Creek.

98. I'm also reminded daily that the great Cherokee civilization was here long before my ancestors came to this beautiful area. Places have names like Choestoe (land of the dancing rabbits), Hiawassee (pretty fawn), Nottley (daring horseman), Enotah (bare), Chatuge (chicken), Ellijay (new ground), Chattahoochee (flowering rocks), Nantahala (land of the noon day sun), and Tesnatee (turkey).

99. Fireplaces, wood stoves, rail fences, honeysuckle.

100. We mountaineers love to look backwards, and there are plenty of places in Appalachia to do that. A few of the centers and institutes include the Archives of Appalachia, Berea College Appalachian Center, Blue Ridge Institute and Museum, and the Folkways Center of the Georgia Mountains.

101. The rugged ridges and isolated valleys that for centuries served as buffers against the encroachment of the outside world have now become not buffers but beacons for an ever-growing invasion of the region. Welcome! But help us not to spoil it. I want future generations to have their 101 reasons why they live in Appalachia.

ZELL MILLER

began his career in public service in 1959 with a term as mayor of Young Harris, Georgia. In 1960, he was elected to the Georgia Senate at the age of 28. In 1974, he won the first of four consecutive terms as Georgia's lieutenant governor. Then in 1990, Miller ran for governor and won the first of two terms he would serve as the state's top leader. From 2000 through 2004, he served as a United States Senator for the state of Georgia.

After a lifetime of politics, teaching, speaking, and writing, including two *New York Times* best sellers, Zell Miller and his wife Shirley retired to his home in Brasstown Valley in the mountains of North Georgia. His books include *The Mountains Within Me*, *A National Party No More*, *A Deficit of Decency*, and *The Miracle of Brasstown Valley*.